Nick Vandome

iPhone
for Seniors

9th edition
covers all iPhones with iOS 16

In easy steps is an imprint of In Easy Steps Limited
16 Hamilton Terrace · Holly Walk · Leamington Spa
Warwickshire · United Kingdom · CV32 4LY
www.ineasysteps.com

Ninth Edition

Notice of Liability
Every effort has been made to ensure that this book contains accurate
and current information. However, In Easy Steps Limited and the
author shall not be liable for any loss or damage suffered by readers
as a result of any information contained herein.

Trademarks
iPhone® is a registered trademark of Apple Computer, Inc. All other
trademarks are acknowledged as belonging to their respective
companies.

In Easy Steps Limited supports The Forest Stewardship Council (FSC),
the leading international forest certification organization. All our titles
that are printed on Greenpeace approved FSC certified paper carry the
FSC logo.

MIX
Paper from
responsible sources
FSC® C020837

Printed and bound in the United Kingdom

ISBN 978-1-84078-982-9

Contents

1 Your New iPhone

The iPhone is a sleek, stylish smartphone that is ideal for anyone, of any age. This chapter introduces the four models of the latest version – the iPhone 14 – and takes you through the controls used to navigate around. It also shows how to set it up.

The **New** icon pictured above indicates a new or enhanced feature introduced with the iPhone 14 and the iPhone 14 Pro, or the latest version of its operating system, iOS 16.

One of the features of all of the iPhone 14 models is that they can be used with 5G networks for mobile data and communication. Check with your service provider whether 5G is available in your area. All iPhone 14 models can also access 4G and 3G networks.

All iPhone models have connectivity for fast 802.11ax Wi-Fi, and Bluetooth 5.3.

Hands on with the iPhone

The iPhone is one of the great success stories of the digital age. It is one of the world's leading smartphones: a touchscreen phone that can be used for not only making calls and sending text messages, but also for online access and a huge range of tasks through the use of apps. Essentially, the iPhone is a powerful, compact computer that can be used for everything you need in your mobile life.

The latest range of iPhones includes the iPhone 14, which is available in two sizes, and the iPhone 14 Pro, which is also available in two sizes. All models use the iOS 16 operating system and the A15 or A16 Bionic chip processor.

iPhone 14

This is the standard iPhone, and its specifications include:

- **Screen**: The iPhone 14 has a **6.1-inch** (measured diagonally) Super Retina XDR display screen.

- **Storage**: This determines how much content you can store on your iPhone. For the iPhone 14, the storage capacity options are: 128GB, 256GB or 512GB.

- **Camera**: A dual-lens 12-megapixel (MP) camera for taking photos, and a front-facing 12MP TrueDepth camera for selfies, videos, and for use with Face ID.

- **Face ID**: Unlock the iPhone by looking at the screen.

- **Battery power**: The iPhone 14 provides up to 80 hours of wireless audio playback, 20 hours' video playback, 16 hours' video streaming, and fast charging capability.

- **Input/Output**: There is a Lightning Connector port (for charging, headphones, and connecting to a computer), a built-in speaker, and a built-in microphone.

- **Water-resistant**: Water-resistant up to six meters for up to 30 minutes. Also, splash- and dust-resistant.

- **Sensors**: The sensors are: accelerometer, barometer, ambient light sensor, proximity sensor, and gyroscope.

iPhone 14 Plus

This is a larger version of the standard iPhone 14. Its specifications include:

- **Screen**: The iPhone 14 Plus has a **6.7-inch** (measured diagonally) Super Retina XDR display screen.

- **Storage**: This determines how much content you can store on your iPhone. For the iPhone 14 Plus, the storage capacity options are: 128GB, 256GB or 512GB.

- **Camera**: A dual-lens 12MP camera for taking photos, and a front-facing 12MP TrueDepth camera for selfies, videos, and for use with Face ID.

- **Face ID**: Unlock the iPhone by looking at the screen.

- **Battery power**: The iPhone 14 Plus provides up to 100 hours of wireless audio playback, 26 hours' video playback, 20 hours' video streaming, and fast charging capability.

- **Input/Output**: There is a Lightning Connector port (for charging, headphones, and connecting to a computer), a built-in speaker, and a built-in microphone.

- **Water-resistant**: Water-resistant up to six meters for up to 30 minutes. Also, splash- and dust-resistant.

- **Sensors**: The sensors are: accelerometer, barometer, ambient light sensor, proximity sensor, and gyroscope.

Beware

The iPhone 14 models do not come with a power adapter or EarPods/earphones. The rationale behind this is that a lot of people already have them from previous models of iPhones, and by not including them, Apple is helping to protect the environment by reducing the number of accessories. However, if you do not have a compatible iPhone power adapter you will need to buy one before you can charge your iPhone. A USB-C to Lightning cable is included with the iPhone, and this can be connected to a compatible power adapter if you have one.

Beware

The amount of storage you need may change once you have bought your iPhone. If possible, buy a version with as much storage as your budget allows, as you cannot add more later.

Don't forget

All of the iPhone 14 models are made with Ceramic Shield glass for the display, which makes them four times more durable than previous iPhones if they are dropped.

Don't forget

None of the latest range of iPhones has a separate headphone jack: this is accommodated using the Lightning Connector port.

...cont'd

iPhone 14 Pro

This is the fourth version of the iPhone with "Pro" in its designation. Its specifications include:

- **Screen**: The iPhone 14 Pro has a **6.1-inch** (measured diagonally) Super Retina XDR display screen.

- **Storage**: This determines how much content you can store on your iPhone. For the iPhone 14 Pro, the storage capacity options are: 128GB, 256GB, 512GB, or 1TB.

- **Camera**: A triple-lens 48MP camera for taking photos, and a front-facing 12MP TrueDepth camera for taking selfies, videos, and for use with Face ID.

- **Face ID**: Unlock the iPhone by looking at the screen.

- **Battery power**: The iPhone 14 Pro provides up to 75 hours of wireless audio playback, 23 hours' video playback, 20 hours' video streaming, and fast charging capability.

- **Input/Output**: There is a Lightning Connector port (for charging, headphones, and connecting to a computer), a built-in speaker, and a built-in microphone.

- **Water-resistant**: Water-resistant up to six meters for up to 30 minutes. Also, splash- and dust-resistant.

- **Sensors**: The sensors are: LiDAR scanner (for using the main camera in Night Mode), accelerometer, barometer, ambient light sensor, proximity sensor, and gyroscope.

iPhone 14 Pro Max

This is a larger version of the iPhone 14 Pro, and has the same camera system and a larger display screen. Its specifications include:

- **Screen**: The iPhone 14 Pro Max has a **6.7-inch** (measured diagonally) Super Retina XDR display screen.

- **Storage**: This determines how much content you can store on your iPhone. For the iPhone 14 Pro Max, the storage capacity options are: 128GB, 256GB, 512GB, or 1TB.

- **Camera**: A triple-lens 48MP camera for taking photos, and a front-facing 12MP TrueDepth camera for taking selfies, videos, and for use with Face ID.

- **Face ID**: Unlock the iPhone by looking at the screen.

- **Battery power**: The iPhone 14 Pro Max provides up to 95 hours of wireless audio playback, 29 hours' video playback, 25 hours' video streaming, and fast charging capability.

- **Input/Output**: There is a Lightning Connector port (for charging, headphones, and connecting to a computer), a built-in speaker, and a built-in microphone.

- **Water-resistant**: Water-resistant up to six meters for up to 30 minutes. Also, splash- and dust-resistant.

- **Sensors**: The sensors are: LiDAR scanner (for using the main camera in Night Mode), accelerometer, barometer, ambient light sensor, proximity sensor, and gyroscope.

Don't forget

The phone services for the iPhone are provided by companies that enable access to their mobile networks, which you will be able to use for phone calls, texts, and mobile data for access to the internet. Companies provide different packages: you can buy the iPhone for a reduced sum and then pay a monthly contract, typically for 12 or 24 months. Despite the fact that the initial outlay for the iPhone will be cheaper, this works out more expensive over the period of the contract. Another option is to buy the iPhone (make sure it is unlocked so that you can use any SIM card) and use a SIM-only offer. This way, you can buy a package that suits you for calls, texts and mobile data. Look for offers that have unlimited data for internet access.

iPhone Nuts and Bolts

On/Off (Side) button

The button for turning the iPhone **On** and **Off** (and putting it into **Sleep** mode) is located on the top right-hand side of the body (looking at the screen). As with other buttons on the body, it is slightly raised to make it easier to locate just by touch.

For more details on turning on the iPhone, see page 16.

Volume controls

Volume is controlled using two separate buttons on the left-hand side of the body. They do not have symbols on them but they are used to increase and decrease the volume.

Buy a glass screen protector to help preserve your iPhone's screen. This will help prevent marks and scratches, and can also save the screen if it is broken: the protector breaks rather than the iPhone's screen itself.

Ringer/silent (use this to turn the ringer **On** or **Off** for when a call or a notification is received)

Volume up button

Volume down button

Top notch (iPhone14 and 14 Plus)

The iPhone 14 and 14 Plus models have a notch at the top of the screen that accommodates the TrueDepth camera, sensors for use with Face ID, built-in stereo speakers, and a built-in microphone.

To make phone calls with your iPhone you need to have an active SIM card inserted, and a suitable service provider for cellular (mobile) calls and data.

The iPhone 14 Pro and 14 Pro Max models have a pill-shaped cutout rather than a top notch; see page 14.

Lightning Connector, speakers and microphone

These are located at the bottom of the iPhone.

Stereo speakers

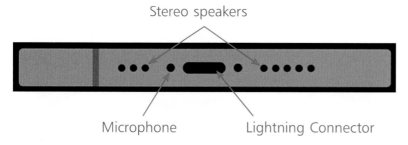

Microphone   Lightning Connector

Back view of the iPhone

This contains the main camera, the LED flash, and the rear microphone.

iPhone 14 and 14 Plus

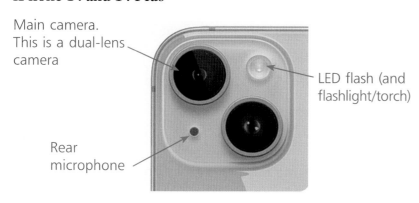

Main camera.
This is a dual-lens camera

LED flash (and flashlight/torch)

Rear microphone

iPhone 14 Pro and 14 Pro Max

The camera on the iPhone 14 Pro and 14 Pro Max has three lenses for the main camera: one ultra-wide-angle, one wide-angle and one telephoto. They combine to take each shot. This produces the highest-quality photos yet on an iPhone, with a range of options such as **Ultra Wide**. See page 110 for more details.

Don't forget

The main camera on all iPhone 14 models can capture excellent photos and also 4K (ultra-high-definition) and high-definition (HD) video. The front-facing TrueDepth camera has a 12MP resolution and can be used for taking "selfies": the modern craze of taking a photo of yourself and then posting it online on a social media site such as Facebook. It is also used for the Face ID functionality for unlocking the iPhone (see page 24), and for FaceTime video calls (see pages 130-135).

13

iPhone 14 Pro Dynamic Island

The Dynamic Island is a new feature on the iPhone, using iOS 16.

Instead of the top notch that is included with the iPhone 14 and 14 Plus models (and has featured on several previous versions of the iPhone), the iPhone 14 Pro and 14 Pro Max have a pill-shaped cutout at the top of the phone's body.

Hot tip

The iPhone 14 models use MagSafe technology to connect a range of accessories, including a wireless charging base station for charging the iPhone. The MagSafe technology includes a designated magnetic area on the back of the iPhone that can be used to attach MagSafe accessories, including a wireless charger and various iPhone cases. There is also a wide range of standard accessories for the iPhone. These include cases in a range of colors and materials.

This contains a front-facing camera and related sensors but it can do much more than take photos. It also displays a range of alerts and notifications, and activities from currently-open apps. Some of the items that can be displayed in the Dynamic Island include:

- Face ID activities; i.e. when you use this to unlock your iPhone, or use it with a compatible app.

- Current timers that are in operation.

- Music playback with the Music app.

- Battery charging status and low battery alerts.

- Incoming phone or FaceTime calls and call durations.

- Directions from the Maps app.

- Switching between silent mode and ring mode.

When a compatible activity is accessed it appears in the Dynamic Island and, in some cases, expands over the Dynamic Island. Tap once on a Dynamic Island item to go to the related app. Press and hold on an item to view a menu of additional options, if there are any. Tap once anywhere on the Home screen to minimize an item in the Dynamic Island.

If there are two active items, they are displayed next to each other in the Dynamic Island.

Inserting the SIM

The SIM card for the iPhone will be provided by your mobile carrier; i.e. the company that provides your cellular phone and data services. Without this, you would still be able to communicate with your iPhone, but only via Wi-Fi and compatible services. A SIM card gives you access to a mobile network too. Some iPhones come with the SIM pre-installed, but you can also insert one yourself. To do this:

1 Use a SIM tool to access the SIM tray on the side of the iPhone

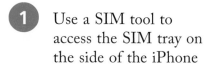

2 Press the tool firmly into the hole on the SIM slot so that the SIM tray pops out and starts to appear. Pull the SIM tray fully out

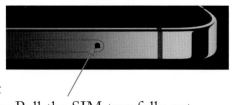

3 Place the SIM card with the metal contacts face downward (shown facing upward in the image). Place the SIM tray in position so that the diagonal cut is in the same position as the cut on the SIM card

4 Place the SIM card on the SIM tray. It should fit flush, resting on a narrow ridge underneath it, with the diagonal cut on the card matching the cut in the SIM tray

5 Place your thumb over the bottom of the SIM tray, covering the SIM card, and place the tray in the SIM slot. Push the tray firmly into the slot until it clicks into place

Beware

The SIM tool is not included with the iPhone 14 models. If you do not have a SIM tool from a previous iPhone, a stretched-out paper clip can be used instead.

Beware

The SIM tray can only be inserted in one way. If it appears to encounter resistance, do not force it; take it out and try again.

Hot tip

All of the iPhone 14 models have dual-SIM capability, which means you can use two separate numbers with the same iPhone.

iPhone Gestures

None of the iPhone 14 models has a **Home** button and, as with the previous range of iPhones, the actions that were previously accessed by pressing the **Home** button are performed by gestures on the screen and actions using the **On/Off** and **Volume** buttons. Gestures for the iPhone include the following (also including some general iPhone actions):

Turning on
Press and hold on the **On/Off** button for a few seconds. Keep it pressed until the Apple icon appears. This will display the Lock screen (see page 23 for details on using the Lock screen).

Unlocking the iPhone
This is done by using Face ID. Once this has been set up (see pages 24-25), raise the phone so that the camera can view your face, and simultaneously swipe up from the bottom of the screen to view the last viewed screen.

Returning to the Home screen
Swipe up from the bar at the bottom of the screen. This can be done from any app.

For iPhones with a **Home** button, press the **Home** button to return to the Home screen from any app.

Hot tip

If your iPhone ever freezes, or if something is not working properly, it can be rebooted by pressing the **Volume up** button, then the **Volume down** button, then pressing and holding the **On/ Off** button.

Beware

The color of the bar at the bottom of the screen, for returning to the Home screen, is dependent on the background color of the app being used. If it has a light background, the bar will be a dark color; if it has a dark background, the bar will be a light color.

Accessing the Control Center

To access the Control Center of useful widgets, swipe down from the top right-hand corner of the screen. (On older iPhone models, this was achieved by swiping up from the bottom of the screen, which now returns you to the Home screen.)

Accessing the Notification Center

The Notification Center is accessed by swiping down from the top left-hand corner or the top middle of the screen.

Accessing Siri

Press and hold the **On/Off** button until Siri appears. Alternatively, use the "Hey Siri" function (see pages 56-57).

Accessing the App Switcher

Swipe up from the bottom of the screen and pause in the middle of the screen to view open and recently-used apps.

Don't forget

Swipe up and down with one finger to move up or down web pages, photos, maps or documents. The content moves in the opposite direction of the swipe; i.e. if you swipe up, the page will move down, and vice versa. Swipe outward with thumb and forefinger to zoom in on a web page, photo, map or document. This enables you to zoom in on an item to a greater degree than when double-tapping with one finger. Pinch together with thumb and forefinger to zoom back out on a web page, photo, map or document.

...cont'd

Reachability

To use **Reachability**, which moves items on the screen to the bottom half to make them easier to access with one hand, swipe down from the bottom of the screen (see page 60 for more details).

Screenshots are saved to the **Photos** app. They can be viewed from the **Photos** button on the bottom toolbar and also from the **Screenshots** album in the **Albums** section.

18

Taking a screenshot

To capture an image of what is currently on the screen, quickly press and release the **On/Off** button and the **Volume up** button simultaneously.

Paying with Apple Pay

To use Apple Pay to pay for items with your iPhone, double-click the **On/Off** button, and authorize with Face ID. See pages 62-63 for details about setting up Apple Pay.

Turning off

Press and hold the **On/Off** button and either of the **Volume** buttons until the Power Off screen appears. Swipe the **slide to power off** button to the right to turn off the iPhone.

Getting Set Up

When you first turn on your iPhone there will be a series of setup screens. These can include some of the following:

- **Language** and **Country**. Select a language and country for where you are using your iPhone.

- **Quick Start**. This can be used to transfer settings from another compatible device, such as an iPad.

- **Choose a Wi-Fi Network**. Connect to the internet, using an available Wi-Fi network.

- **Data & Privacy**. This is used to identify features that ask for your personal information.

- **Face ID**. Use this to create a Face ID for unlocking your iPhone with a scan of your face.

- **Create a Passcode**. This can be used to create a numerical passcode for unlocking your iPhone.

- **Apps & Data**. This can be used to set up an iPhone from an iCloud backup, or as a new iPhone.

- **Apple ID and iCloud**. This can be used to use an existing iCloud account or create a new one.

- **Make this your new iPhone**. If you are setting up from an iCloud backup, this can be used to specify that the iPhone being set up is a new one.

- **Keep your iPhone Up to Date**. This can be used to install updates to the operating system (iOS) automatically.

- **iMessages & FaceTime**. This enables people to contact you using your phone number and email address.

- **Location Services**. This allows apps to use your current locations, such as the Maps app.

- **Siri**. This is used to set up Siri, the digital voice assistant, and dictation options.

- **Screen Time**. This can be used to show how much you use your iPhone and to add restrictions.

Most of the options available during the setup process can also be accessed within the **Settings** app (see pages 20-21).

For more information about using iCloud, see Chapter 3.

Some of the other setup options include: **Analytics**, for sending information from your iPhone that can be used by Apple and developers; **Appearance**, for selecting a **Light** or **Dark** theme; and **Display Zoom**, for specifying the size of icons on the screen.

iPhone Settings

The Settings app controls settings for the way the iPhone and its apps operate:

- **Apple ID, iCloud, Media & Purchases**. Contains settings for these items.

- **Airplane Mode**. This can be used to disable network connectivity while on an airplane.

- **Wi-Fi**. This enables you to select a wireless network.

- **Bluetooth**. Turn this **On** to connect Bluetooth devices.

- **Cellular (Mobile) Data**. These are the settings that will be used with your cellular (mobile) service provider.

- **Personal Hotspot**. This can be used to share your internet connection.

- **Notifications**. This determines how the Notification Center operates (see pages 50-51).

- **Sounds & Haptics**. This has options for setting sounds for alerts, and actions such as tapping on the keyboard.

- **Focus**. Use this to specify times when you do not want to receive audio alerts, phone calls, and video calls.

- **Screen Time**. Options for reporting on and limiting iPhone usage.

- **General**. This contains a range of common settings.

- **Control Center**. This determines how the Control Center operates (see pages 46-49).

- **Display & Brightness**. This can be used to set the screen brightness, text size, and bold text.

- **Home Screen**. This determines how apps are shown on the Home screen and in the App Library.

- **Accessibility**. This can be used for users with visual or motor issues.

The **Cellular (Mobile) Data** settings contain the **Data Roaming** option (**Settings** > **Cellular** > **Cellular Data Options**): if you are traveling abroad you may want to turn this **Off** to avoid undue charges when connected to the internet.

The **Display & Brightness** setting has an option for **Dark Mode**, which inverts the screen color. To use Dark Mode, tap the **Dark** button **On**. To specify when Dark Mode is activated, drag the **Automatic** button **On**, or tap once on the **Options** button to specify a time for Dark Mode.

...cont'd

- **Wallpaper**. This can be used to select a wallpaper.

- **Siri & Search**. Options for the digital voice assistant.

- **Face ID & Passcode**. This has options for adding a passcode or fingerprint ID for unlocking the iPhone.

- **Emergency SOS**. This can be used to set an Auto Call to an emergency number.

- **Battery**. This can be used to view battery usage by apps.

- **Privacy & Security**. This can be used for Location Services so that your location can be used by specific apps.

- **App Store**. This can be used to specify downloading options for the App Store.

- **Wallet & Apple Pay**. This can be used to add credit or debit cards for use with Apple Pay (see pages 62-63).

- **Passwords**. This contains options for managing website passwords.

- **Mail**, **Contacts**, **Calendars**. These are three separate settings that have options for how these apps operate.

iPhone app settings

Most of the built-in iPhone apps have their own settings that determine how the apps operate. These include: Notes, Reminders, Voice Memos, Phone, Messages, FaceTime, Safari, News, Stocks, Weather, Translate, Maps, Compass, Measure, Shortcuts, Health, Music, TV, Photos, Camera, Books, and Podcasts. Tap on one of these tabs to view the settings for that app. (Apps that are downloaded from the App Store also have their individual settings in this location in the Settings app.)

If a settings option has an **On/Off** button next to it, this can be changed by swiping the button to either the left or right. Green indicates that the option is **On**. Select **Settings > Accessibility > Display & Text Size > On/Off Labels** to show or hide icons on each button.

Tap on a link to see additional options.

Tap once here to move back to the previous page for the selected setting:

iOS 16 is the latest operating system for the iPhone.

You will need an Apple ID for all Apple online services. This is free – to register go to https://appleid. apple.com

Tap on **Create Your Apple ID**. You will be prompted to enter your email address and a password. Then, follow the onscreen instructions. Tap on **Create Apple ID** when ready.

To check the version of iOS, look in **Settings > General > Software Update**.

About iOS 16

iOS 16 is the latest version of the operating system for Apple's iPhone range, including all of the latest iPhone 14 models.

iOS 16 further enhances the user experience for which the mobile operating system is renowned. This includes:

- **Customizing the Lock screen**. The iPhone Lock screen can now be customized, with different backgrounds, editable fonts and adding widgets.

- **Shared photo library**. In conjunction with the iCloud online backup and sharing service, a photo library can be created that can be shared with family and friends. Everyone who has access to the library can edit all of the photos within it, and photos can also be added to it directly from the Camera app when they are captured.

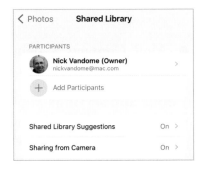

- **Editing text messages**. iMessage text messages to other iOS 16 users can be edited after they have been sent, to correct any typos or mistakes.

- **Unsending text messages and emails**. Both iMessages and emails can be unsent so that they can be retrieved if they are sent in error or contain content that you did not mean to include.

Using the Lock Screen

To save power, it is possible to set your iPhone screen to auto-lock. This is the equivalent of the **Sleep** option on a traditional computer. To do this:

1 Tap once on the **Settings** app

2 Tap once on the **Display & Brightness** tab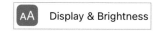

3 Tap once on the **Auto-Lock** option

Auto-Lock	Never >

4 Tap once on the time of non-use after which you wish the screen to be locked

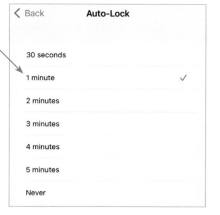

5 Once the screen is locked, look at the screen – if you have Face ID set up (see page 24) – and swipe up from the bottom of the Lock screen to unlock the screen

The screen can also be locked by pressing once on the **On/Off** button on the right-hand side of the iPhone's body.

For details about customizing the Lock screen, see pages 40-43.

Swipe from right to left on the Lock screen to access the camera.

Face ID and Passcode

Since the iPhone models released in 2018, the means of unlocking the phone is done through the use of Face ID. If this cannot be used for any reason, a passcode can be entered instead. To set up Face ID:

1 Select **Settings** > **Face ID & Passcode**

2 Tap once on the **Set Up Face ID** button

Set Up Face ID

3 Position your face in the center of the circle that accesses the iPhone's camera. Move your head slowly in a circle so that the camera can record all elements of your face

Move your head slowly to complete the circle.

4 Tap once on the **Continue** button after the first scan. A second scan will be done to complete the process

First Face ID scan complete.

Continue

5 Tap once on the **Done** button to finish the Face ID setup process

Face ID Is Now Set Up

Done

Hot tip

Face ID can also be used for contactless purchases for Apple Pay (see pages 62-63), and purchases in the iTunes Store and App Store. Drag the buttons **On** as required under the **Use Face ID For:** heading in the **Face ID & Passcode** settings.

24

...cont'd

Adding a passcode
If Face ID cannot be used to unlock the iPhone, a numerical passcode can be used instead. This has to be set up at the same time as creating a Face ID. To do this:

1 Select **Settings** > **Face ID & Passcode**

 Face ID & Passcode

2 Tap once on the **Turn Passcode On** button

< Settings   **Face ID & Passcode**

Turn Passcode On

Change Passcode

Require Passcode   Immediately >

3 Enter a six-digit passcode. This can be used to unlock your iPhone from the Lock screen

Set Passcode   Cancel

Enter a passcode

Passcode Options

1	2 ABC	3 DEF
4 GHI	5 JKL	6 MNO
7 PQRS	8 TUV	9 WXYZ
	0	⌫

4 Once a passcode

Require Passcode   Immediately >

has been created, tap once on the **Require Passcode** button in Step 2 to specify a time period until the passcode is required on the Lock screen. The best option is **Immediately**, otherwise someone else could access your iPhone

Beware

If you use a passcode to lock your iPhone, write it down but store it in a location away from the iPhone.

Don't forget

Tap once on the **Passcode Options** link in Step 3 to access other options for creating a passcode. These include **Custom Alphanumeric Code**, **Custom Numeric Code**, and **4-Digit Code**. The **4-Digit Code** option is the least secure and the **Alphanumeric Code** option is the most secure, as it can use a combination of numbers, letters and symbols.

25

Opening and Closing Apps

One of the first things you will want to do with your iPhone is explore the apps on the Home screen. The good news is that all apps on your iPhone can be opened with the minimum of fuss and effort.

Don't forget

The Home screen is the one that you see when you turn on your iPhone.

Don't forget

You can open as many apps as you like from the Home screen, without needing to close any. However, apps can be closed from the App Switcher (see the next page).

1 Tap once on an icon on the Home screen to open the app

2 The app opens at its own Home screen

3 Swipe up from the bottom of the screen to return to the iPhone Home screen

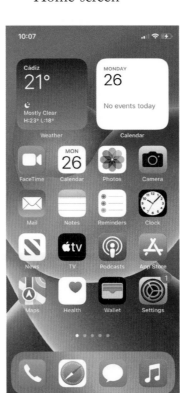

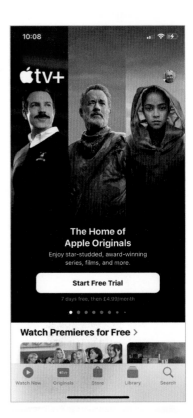

Closing apps

Apps remain open in the background when they are not being used. This uses very little power and they can be left in this state of hibernation until they are needed again. However, apps can also be closed using the App Switcher.

When you switch from one app to another, the first one stays open in the background. You can go back to it by accessing it from the App Switcher window or the Home screen.

1 Swipe up from the bottom of the screen and pause in the middle of the screen to access the App Switcher. From the App Switcher window, swipe left and right between open apps, and tap on one to make it the active app

When an app is closed in the App Switcher window, the other apps move along to fill in the space from the closed app.

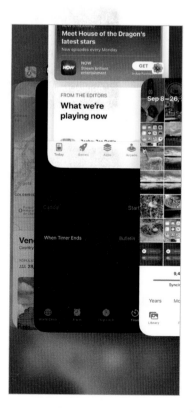

2 Swipe an app to the top of the window in the App Switcher to close it

Swipe up from the bottom of the screen, or tap once on a free area of the App Switcher window, to return to the Home screen.

Updating Software

The operating system that powers the iPhone is known as iOS. This is a mobile computing operating system, and the latest version is iOS 16. Periodically, there are updates to iOS to fix bugs and add new features. These can be downloaded to your iPhone once they are released.

1 Tap once on the **Settings** app

2 If there is an update available, tap once on the **Software Update Available** button (or select **General** > **Software Update** to check for updates)

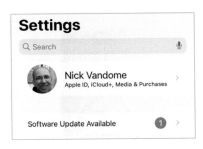

3 The update will be displayed here, with details of what is contained within it

4 Tap once on the **Download and Install** button to start the downloading process. The iOS update will then be done automatically

2 Starting to Use your iPhone

This chapter covers the functions on the iPhone that you need to use it confidently and make the most of its features. From opening and closing apps, using the App Library and Home screens for accessing apps, using the Dock and the Control Center, to managing notifications, it explains the iPhone interface so that you can quickly get up and running with it.

Home Screens

The first thing that you see when your iPhone is turned on is the Home screen. This is where the iPhone's apps are displayed. By default, there is one Home screen, containing the built-in apps. However, as more apps are added, additional Home screens are created to display them.

Hot tip

Swipe to the end of the Home screens to access the App Library (see the next page).

Hot tip

On the first Home screen, swipe to the right, from the left-hand side of the screen, to access the Today View panel widgets (see page 39).

Hot tip

Apps on a Home screen can be opened by tapping on them once.

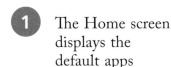 **1** The Home screen displays the default apps

2 As more apps are added, additional Home screens are created to accommodate them. Swipe left and right to move between the available Home screens

App Library

In previous versions of iOS, numerous Home screens could be added, and folders created to contain apps of similar categories. This can still be done in iOS 16, but there is also an option for consolidating the number of Home screens, through the use of the App Library. This can be used to display a page with all of the apps on your iPhone, without a need for numerous different Home screens. To access the App Library:

1 Swipe from right to left until you reach the final Home screen (this is indicated by the small dots at the bottom of the Home screen)

2 Swipe from right to left to access the App Library

Several Home screens can be used as well as the App Library. However, the App Library can be used to make the overall use of your iPhone more streamlined, by removing Home screens so that there are fewer screens to swipe through to view all of your apps.

Working with Home Screens

The App Library is most effective when there are no additional Home screens, apart from the first one, so that all of the apps can be accessed from the App Library. This is done by hiding the existing Home screens. To do this:

1 Press and hold anywhere on a Home screen, to access the control buttons

2 The number of Home screens in use is denoted by this bar toward the bottom of the screen

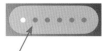

3 Tap once on the Home screen buttons bar to access the editing area

Hot tip

The number of dots on the Home screen buttons bar indicates the number of available Home screens and the App Library, which is denoted by the dot at the far right-hand side of the bar. So, the example in Step 3 includes five Home screens and the App Library.

4 The editing area displays all currently-available Home screens

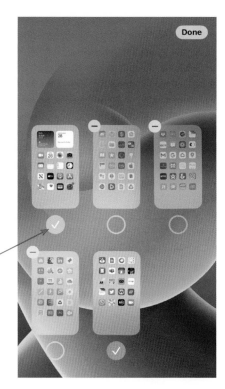

5 Tap once here to select or deselect a Home screen

Hot tip

If the check mark symbol is visible below a Home screen, this means that the Home screen will be available.

6 At least one Home screen has to be selected, but it can be any of the available options

Don't forget

Once a Home screen has been hidden, the apps within it will not be visible, but they can be accessed from the App Library.

7 Tap once on the **Done** button to apply the Home screen changes, and tap

Done

once on the **Done** button on the Home screen to complete the editing process

Using the App Library

The App Library automatically arranges apps into folders, based on their categories. Apps can be opened and deleted directly from the App Library. To use the App Library to work with and manage the apps on your iPhone:

Beware

The order of the folders in the App Library cannot be changed; i.e. you cannot move them around within the App Library.

1 Move to the final Home screen in use. This is indicated by the dots toward the bottom of the Home screen. (If there is only one Home screen in use there will not be any dots showing unless the Home screen controls are accessed, as shown on page 32)

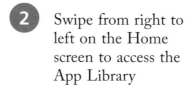

2 Swipe from right to left on the Home screen to access the App Library

3 Apps in the App Library are automatically organized into appropriate folders. Tap once on an app in a folder to open it

4 If a folder has four or fewer apps, they are all displayed. If there are more than four apps, tap once on the bottom right-hand corner of a folder to view all of the apps within it

5 Press and hold anywhere on the App Library page to access the control buttons

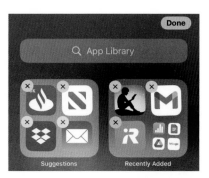

6 Tap once on this button to delete an app from your iPhone

Viewing apps

To view all of the apps in the App Library:

1 Swipe downward anywhere within the App Library

2 All available apps are listed alphabetically

3 Swipe up and down to view all of the available apps, or tap on the alphabetic sidebar to move to that section

4 Use the Search box at the top of the App Library window to search for specific apps. As you type, matching apps will appear below the Search box

Beware

When an app is deleted as in Step 6, a confirmation dialog box will ask if you want to delete the app. Tap once on the **Delete** button if you do. Deleted apps can be reinstated from the App Store at any time.

Don't forget

Apps can be deleted from a Home screen in the same way as deleting them in the App Library.

Hot tip

The more letters used in the Search box in Step 4, the more defined the search results will become. For instance, "ca" will produce more results than "cal".

Widgets on the Home Screen

The iPhone Home screen contains icons for the apps that can be accessed, and also widgets containing items of useful information, which are located at the top of the Home screen.

By default, these widgets are displayed in two stacks (several widgets together), initially displaying the Weather widget and the Calendar widget.

Press and hold anywhere on the Home screen to access the editing controls for the widgets.

To use widgets on the Home screen:

1   Tap once on a widget, or a stack, to open the full version of the app

2   Swipe up or down on a stack to view other widgets within it

3 Tap once on the active widget in a stack to open the full version of the app

4 Press and hold a stack or a widget to access its own menu options

Moving widgets

Stacks and widgets on the Home screen can be moved around so that you can order them how you want. To do this:

1 Press and hold on an item on the Home screen until the controls appear

2 Drag the item into a new position. Stacks and widgets remain at their selected sizes, and other items will be reordered to accommodate the moved widget accordingly

Removing Home screen stacks and widgets

Stacks and widgets on the Home screen can be removed from the Home screen. To do this:

1 Press and hold on a item until its menu appears. Tap once on the **Remove Stack** or **Remove Widget** button

2 Tap once on the **Remove** button

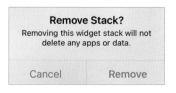

Remove Stack?
Removing this widget stack will not delete any apps or data.

Cancel   Remove

...cont'd

Adding Home screen stacks and widgets

Items on the Home screen can be customized to display different apps and at different sizes. To do this:

Don't forget

If all widgets are removed from the Home screen, the apps on the Home screen will be rearranged to take up the available space. If widgets are then reinstated, they will take up their original position on the Home screen.

Don't forget

Some widgets can be edited, depending on their functionality. To do this, press and hold on a widget to access its menu. Tap once on the **Edit Widget** button, if this is available.

1 Press and hold on the Home screen items until they start to wobble (or, if they have been removed, press and hold anywhere on the Home screen)

2 Tap once on the **+** button in the top left-hand corner

3 The Widgets Library is displayed. The main panel contains suggested widgets to use. The **Search Widgets** box at the top of the window can be used to search for specific widgets

4 Tap once on a widget to view options for adding it to the Home screen. Swipe from right to left, or tap on the dots toward the bottom of the window, to access the different sizes and formats at which the widget can be used

5 Tap once on the **Add Widget** button. The widget is added to the Home screen, at the size selected in Step 4

Today View Panel

The Today View panel contains similar widgets to the Home screen, but they are not displayed on the Home screen. To use the Today View panel:

1 Swipe from left to right on the left-hand edge of the Home screen to access the Today View panel, which contains the Today View widgets

2 Press and hold anywhere within the Today View panel to access its editing controls. Tap once on the **+** button to add more widgets. Tap once on the **−** button to remove a widget

Hot tip

Tap once on the **Customize** button, accessed from the **Edit** button in Step 3, to access options for adding widgets to the Today View panel.

3 Swipe up on the Today View panel to see all widgets currently in it. Tap once on the **Edit** button at the bottom of the Today View panel to access the editing controls for the widgets, including the **Customize** option – see the Hot tip

Edit

Customizing the Lock Screen

Customizing the Lock screen is a new feature in iOS 16.

The Lock screen can be activated by pressing the **On/Off** button on the side of the iPhone once. It can also be accessed by swiping down from the top middle of any screen being viewed.

The Focus function can be added to the Lock screen by tapping once on the **Focus** button in Step 1. See pages 52-55 for more details about using the Focus function.

In previous versions of iOS, the purpose of the Lock screen was primarily a security feature, to prevent unauthorized access to an iPhone. However, in iOS 16 the functionality of the Lock screen has been increased considerably. Elements on the Lock screen can now be customized in terms of changing the background, editing font and color, and adding widgets to the Lock screen so that their information can be viewed without having to unlock the iPhone.

Customizing elements

To customize existing elements of the Lock screen:

1. Activate the Lock screen and press and hold on it to access the customization options. (Swipe left or right to view the different Lock screen options and tap once on one to apply it as the current Lock screen)

2. Tap once on the **Customize** button

3. Tap once on the date or time box

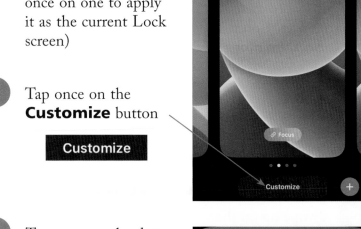

4 Select new fonts and colors for the date and time boxes, as required

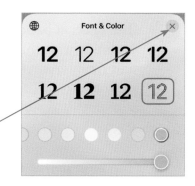

5 Tap once on the cross in the top right-hand corner of the **Font & Color** window to close it. Any changes that have been made will be applied to the text

6 Tap once on the **Done** button

Options for changing the Lock screen background can also be accessed from the initial customization screen; see page 42.

41

Changing the background

To change the background of the Lock screen:

1 Activate the customization options as shown in Step 1 on the previous page and tap once on this button

2 The available background options are displayed

3 Swipe from right to left to view more available background options

4 Tap once on a background to select it

Hot tip

Swipe from right to left on the **Suggested Photos** option to see more photos from your own photo library that can be used as the Lock screen background.

...cont'd

5 The selected background is shown with the date and time boxes. Tap once on these to edit them, if required, as shown on page 40

6 Tap once on the **Done** button to apply the existing Lock screen background

Done

Hot tip

Tap once on the **Customize Home Screen** button in Step 7 to apply a background to the Home screen that is different from the Lock screen one.

7 Tap once on the **Set as Wallpaper Pair** button to apply the background to the Lock screen and the Home screen

8 The option for changing the Lock screen background can also be accessed from Step 1 on page 40 by swiping from right to left and tapping once on the **Add New** button

Adding widgets

Specific widgets can also be added to the Lock screen, to give it increased functionality. To do this:

1 Activate the customization options as shown in Step 1 on page 40 and tap once in the box below the time box (the widgets box)

2 Tap once on a widget in the **Add Widgets** window to add it to the widgets box. Tap once on the - icon to remove a widget

A maximum of four widgets can be added to the Lock screen, or fewer, depending on the size of the widget.

43

3 Once the required widgets have been added, tap once on the **Done** button. The widgets will now appear on the Lock screen

Using the Dock

By default, there are four apps on the Dock at the bottom of the iPhone's screen. These are the four that Apple thinks you will use most frequently:

Hot tip

With iOS 16, some of the pre-installed (built-in) apps can be deleted from your iPhone. These are indicated by a – symbol in the top left-hand corner when you press and hold on an app.

- **Phone**, for making and receiving calls.

- **Safari**, for web browsing.

- **Messages**, for text messaging.

- **Music**.

You can rearrange the order in which the Dock apps appear.

Hot tip

Just above the Dock is a line of small dots. These indicate how many screens of content there are on the iPhone. Tap on one of the dots to go to that screen. (If the App Library is being used instead of separate Home screens – see pages 34-35 – there will only be two dots.)

1 Press and hold on one of the Dock apps until it starts to jiggle

2 Drag the app into its new position

3 Swipe up from the bottom of the screen to exit editing mode

44

Adding and removing Dock apps

You can also remove apps from the Dock and add new ones.

1 To remove an app from the Dock, press and hold it, and drag it onto the main screen area

Don't forget

If items are removed from the Dock they are still available in the same way from the main screen.

2 To add an app to the Dock, press and hold it, and drag it onto the Dock

Hot tip

3 The number of items that can be added to the Dock is restricted to a maximum of four, as the icons do not resize

Editing mode can also be exited by tapping on the **Done** button in the top right-hand corner of the screen.

Done

4 Swipe up from the bottom of the screen to exit editing mode

45

Using the Control Center

The Control Center is a panel containing some of the most commonly-used options within the **Settings** app.

Accessing the Control Center
The Control Center can be accessed with one swipe from any screen within iOS 16, and it can also be accessed from the Lock screen. To set this up:

1 Tap once on the **Settings** app

2 Tap once on the **Control Center** tab, and drag the **Access Within Apps** button **On** or **Off** to specify if the Control Center can be accessed from there (if it is **Off**, it can still be accessed from any Home screen)

3 Swipe down from the top right-hand corner of any screen to access the Control Center

Control Center functionality
The Control Center contains items that have differing formats and functionality. To access these:

1 Press and hold on the folder of four icons in the top left-hand corner, to access the **Airplane Mode**, **Cellular Data**, **Wi-Fi**, **Bluetooth**, **AirDrop**, and **Personal Hotspot** options

Don't forget

AirDrop is the functionality for sharing items wirelessly between compatible devices. Tap once on the **AirDrop** button in the Control Center and specify whether you want to share with **Receiving Only**, **Contacts Only** or **Everyone**. Once AirDrop is set up, you can use the **Share** button in compatible apps to share items such as photos with any other AirDrop users in the vicinity.

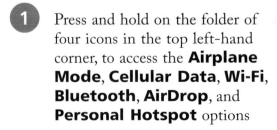

2 Press on this button to expand
the options for music controls,
including playing or pausing items
and changing the volume. Tap once
on this icon to send music from
your iPhone to other compatible
devices, such as AirPod headphones or HomePods,
Apple's wireless speakers

3 Tap once on individual
buttons to turn items **On**
or **Off** (they change color
depending on their state)

The Control Center
cannot be disabled
from being accessed
from the Home screen.

4 Drag on these items to increase or decrease the
screen brightness and the volume

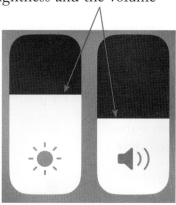

Hot tip

Bluetooth can be used to connect to other compatible devices, using radio waves over short distances up to approximately 20 meters. Both devices must have Bluetooth turned **On** and be "paired" with each other. This links them together so that content such as photos can be shared between them.

Don't forget

Press and hold on the **Camera** button to access options for taking a "selfie" (a self-portrait), recording a video, taking a portrait or taking a portrait selfie.

...cont'd

Control Center controls

Access the items in the Control Center as follows:

- Tap once on this button to turn **Airplane Mode** On or Off, for network connections.

- Tap once on this button to turn **Cellular Data** On or Off, for cellular networks.

- Tap once on this button to turn **Wi-Fi** On or Off.

- Tap once on this button to turn **Bluetooth** On or Off.

- Tap once on this button to activate **AirDrop** for sharing items with other AirDrop users.

- Tap once on this button to turn **Personal Hotspot** On or Off, to use your iPhone as a hotspot for connecting another device like an iPad or Mac computer to the internet.

- Tap once on this button to **Lock** or **Unlock** screen rotation. If it is locked, the screen will not change when you change the orientation.

- Tap once on this button to access **Focus** mode (see pages 52-55).

- Tap once on this button to turn on the **Flashlight/Torch** item. Press on the button to change the intensity of the flashlight/torch.

- Tap once on this button to access the **Clock** item, including a stopwatch and timer. Press on the button to access a scale for creating reminders.

- Tap once on this button to open the **Calculator** app.

- Tap once on this button to open the **Camera** app.

Customizing the Control Center

The Control Center can be customized so that items can be added or removed. To do this:

1 Tap once on the **Settings** app

2 Tap once on the **Control Center** tab

3 Drag the **Access Within Apps** button **On**, to enable the Control Center to be accessed from any open app

4 Items currently in the Control Center are shown at the top of the window; those that can be added are below them. Tap once on a red icon to remove an existing item, or tap once on a green icon to add new items to the Control Center

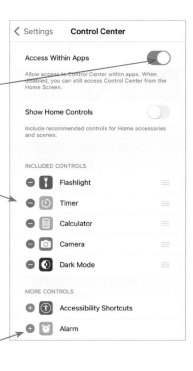

5 Items that are added in Step 4 are included in the Control Center, and can be accessed from here

Hot tip

Dark Mode can be activated by tapping on this button in the Control Center:

If the button is not visible by default in the Control Center, access **Settings** > **Control Center** and tap once on the green **+** button next to **Dark Mode**.

Hot tip

The flashlight/torch and the camera can both be accessed directly from buttons on the Lock screen too.

Hot tip

The Notification Center can be accessed by dragging down from the top left-hand corner or the middle of the screen, in any app.

Don't forget

Use Scheduled Summary (tap once on the **Scheduled Summary** button in the main **Notifications** window) to specify settings for grouping notifications and displaying them at a specific time.

Notifications

Although the Notification Center feature is not an app in its own right, it can be used to display information from a variety of apps. The notifications appear as a list of all items you want to be reminded about or be made aware of. Notifications are set up within the Settings app. To do this:

1 Tap once on the **Settings** app

2 Tap once on the **Notifications** tab

3 In the **Notification Style** section, tap once on an item to determine how it operates when it displays a notification

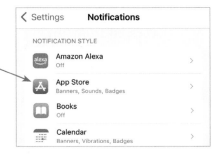

4 Drag the **Allow Notifications** button **On** to allow notifications to be displayed for this item

5 Make selections for how you want the notification to appear. This includes the Lock screen, the Notification Center and as an onscreen banner

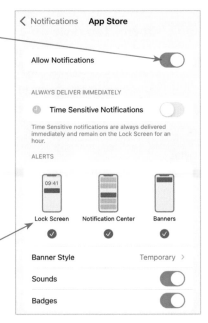

6 Drag the **Time Sensitive Notifications** button **On** to enable notifications to be displayed as soon as they become active, if they are time-specific – e.g. for a calendar event at a specific time

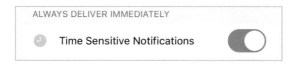

Viewing notifications

Once the Notifications settings have been selected, they can be used to keep up-to-date with all of your important appointments and reminders, via the Notification Center. To view the Notification Center:

1 Drag down from the top of any screen to view the Notification Center. This displays items that have been selected, as shown on the previous page. Tap once on an item to open it in its own app

2 If the **Time Sensitive Notifications** option has been turned **On**, as in Step 6 above, there are options to **Leave On** or **Turn Off**

Hot tip

For each app that has had notifications turned **On**, there is an option to group the notifications so that they are all displayed together in the Notification Center. To do this, access the required app in the Notifications settings and tap once on the **Notifications Grouping** option to specify how these are displayed.

Focus

Another option for managing your notifications is the **Focus** function, which can be used to control when you are notified about certain items. The Focus function can be used to limit notifications when you are performing certain actions (e.g. reading or relaxing) and it can also specify certain people and apps that are allowed to contact you and send notifications. The Focus function can be set up within the Settings app, and also accessed from the Control Center. To do this:

52

1 Tap once on the **Settings** app

2 Tap once on the **Focus** tab

3 Tap once on the **+** button in the top right-hand corner

4 A range of options for setting a Focus is displayed. Tap once on one – e.g. the **Personal** option

5 Tap once on the **Customize Focus** button

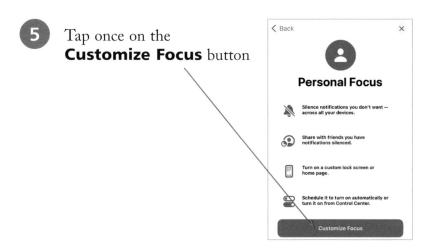

6 Tap once on the **People** button, to add someone from whom notifications can still appear

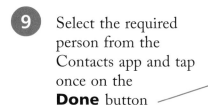

If you add too many people in Step 6, this could negate the effect of using the specific Focus.

7 Tap once on the **Allow Notifications From** option

8 Tap once on the **Add People** button

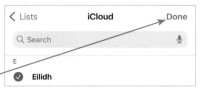

9 Select the required person from the Contacts app and tap once on the **Done** button

...cont'd

10 Select options for allowed calls during the Focus and tap once on the **Done** button. The person selected in Step 9 on page 53 is added to the Focus

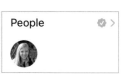

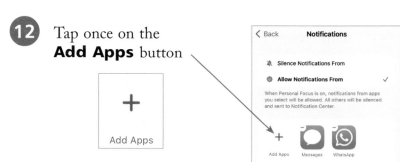

Beware

If you select **Everybody** in Step 10 for allowed calls, no calls will be restricted, regardless of other options within the Focus.

11 Tap once on the **Apps** button in Step 6 on page 53

12 Tap once on the **Add Apps** button

13 Select apps to be included in the Focus – i.e. you will be able to receive notifications from them – and tap once on the **Done** button

14 The selected app is added to the Focus. Tap once on the **Back** button to view the full details of the Focus

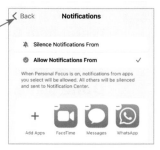

15 Details about the Focus are displayed in the **Focus** section of the Settings app. Tap once on the **Focus** button to return to the main Focus page, where you can view all currently-active Focuses

16 Details of Focuses can be accessed from the Control Center, by tapping on the **Focus** button. Drag down from the top right-hand corner of any window to access the Control Center and tap once on this button (if a Focus has not been set up, the button will display **Focus**)

Tap once on the menu button on a Focus in Step 17 to access options for applying how long the Focus is activated for.

17 Details of any Focus settings are displayed. Tap once on a Focus to turn it **On** or **Off**, or tap once on the **New Focus** button to create a new one

Setting Up Siri

Siri is the iPhone's voice assistant that provides answers to a variety of verbal questions by looking at content in your iPhone and also web services. You can ask Siri questions relating to the apps on your iPhone, and also general questions such as weather conditions around the world or sports results. Initially, Siri can be set up within the **Settings** app.

Siri can be used to translate English words or phrases into different languages.

1 Tap once on the **Settings** app

2 Tap once on the **Siri & Search** tab

Options for Siri

Within the Siri settings there are options for its operation.

1 Drag the **Listen for "Hey Siri"** button **On** if you want to be able to access Siri just by saying **Hey Siri**

2 Make selections here for the language, voice type, feedback and your own details to use with Siri

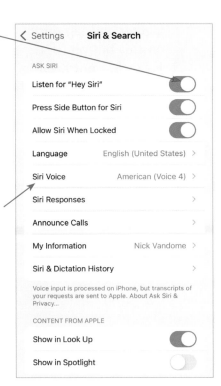

3 If using "Hey Siri", it has to be set up by training it for your voice. Tap once on the **Continue** button

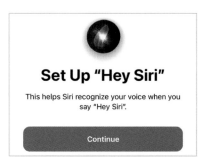

Set Up "Hey Siri"
This helps Siri recognize your voice when you say "Hey Siri".

Continue

Hot tip

Siri can be used to open any of the pre-installed iPhone apps, simply by saying **Open Photos**, for example.

4 Repeat the range of phrases to train Siri to your voice. This is a five-step process

Say "Hey Siri" into your iPhone

Hot tip

Whenever you access a feature that uses your iPhone's microphone, such as asking a question of Siri or recording a voice memo, a small orange dot appears at the top of the screen to indicate that an app has accessed the microphone. This is a security feature so that you can see if anything has accessed your microphone when you do not expect it.

5 Tap once on the **Done** button to complete the "Hey Siri" setup

"Hey Siri" Is Ready
Siri will recognize your voice whenever you say, "Hey Siri".

Done

Accessing Siri
To access Siri:

1 Press and hold the **On/Off** button until the Siri screen appears, or say "Hey Siri"

2 The Siri icon appears at the bottom of the screen. Ask your question to Siri. After the reply, tap once on this icon to ask another question

57

Siri can also display specific contacts. Say **Show me...** followed by the person's name to view their details (if they are in your contacts – see pages 78-79).

Hot tip

Siri can also read out your information: open an item such as a calendar appointment and then say **Read appointment**.

Don't forget

You can ask for weather forecasts for specific periods such as **Today** or **This Week**. However, Siri's power of forecasting only stretches to 10 days in the future.

Finding Things with Siri

Siri is very versatile and can be used for a wide range of functions, including finding things on your iPhone, searching the web, getting weather forecasts, finding locations, and even playing music.

Accessing your apps

To use Siri to find things on your iPhone:

1 Access Siri as shown on page 57

2 To find something from your iPhone apps, say something such as **Open my contacts**

3 The requested app is displayed

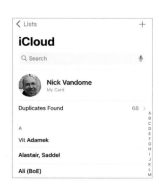

Getting the weather

You can ask Siri for weather forecasts for locations around the world. Simply ask for the weather in a certain city or location. The current weather details are displayed. Tap once on the weather details to view a more extensive forecast.

Finding locations

Siri is also effective for viewing locations within the Maps app. This can be done on an international, national or city level. Siri can also be used to get directions.

Searching locally

If Location Services is turned **On** for Siri, then you can ask for local information such as **Show the nearest Italian restaurants**. Siri can also be used to call restaurants and provide directions.

Playing music

You can use Siri to play any of the music that you have in the Music app. Simply ask Siri to play a track and it will start playing. (Music can be downloaded from the iTunes Store app; see pages 150-152 for more details.) To stop a song, simply say **Stop playing**.

Siri can be used with certain third-party apps to perform tasks such as booking a taxi or a restaurant table.

Items can also be searched for using the **Spotlight Search** option. This can be accessed by swiping downward on the Home screen and entering a keyword or phrase in the Search box at the top of the window. Items can be searched for on your iPhone (including apps) and over the web.

59

Siri can also play a whole album as well as individual music tracks.

Reachability

Because of the size of the iPhone 14, the iPhone 14 Plus, the iPhone 14 Pro, and the iPhone 14 Pro Max, it is not always easy to access all items with one hand. This is overcome by a feature known as **Reachability**, which can be accessed from any screen of the iPhone. This moves items on the screen to the bottom half, and they can all be accessed from here.

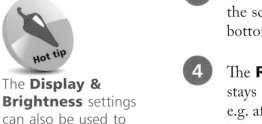

Hot tip

If the **Reachability** function is not turned **On** by default, go to **Settings** > **Accessibility** > **Touch** and drag the **Reachability** button **On**.

1 By default, all items on the screen take up the whole area

2 Swipe down on the bottom edge of the screen

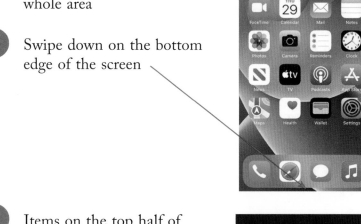

3 Items on the top half of the screen are moved to the bottom half

4 The **Reachability** effect stays in place for one action; e.g. after you tap on an item, the screen reverts to normal size

Hot tip

The **Display & Brightness** settings can also be used to increase the text size for supported apps. Tap once on the **Text Size** button to access a slider with which you can set the required text size.

Night Shift

Getting a good night's sleep is becoming increasingly recognized as a vital and often-overlooked element of our overall health and wellbeing. One of the biggest obstacles to this is the amount of artificial lighting that we experience at night time, such as street lighting, lighting in the home, and the light emitted from mobile devices such as iPhones. This type of light is known as "blue light", and it is one of the most restrictive in terms of getting a good night's sleep as it is the type of light that instructs the body that it is time to be awake and alert. One option to reduce the impact of blue light from your iPhone is to use the **Night Shift** option, which reduces the amount of blue light that is emitted.

Try not to use your iPhone or other mobile devices for prolonged periods just before you go to bed, to reduce the amount of artificial light that you are experiencing. Also, it is best to turn off your iPhone when you go to bed, as it is a good way to suggest to your brain that it is time for sleep.

1 Tap once on the **Settings** app

2 Tap once on the **Display & Brightness** tab

3 Tap once on the **Night Shift** button

4 Drag the **Scheduled** button **On** and tap once on the **From/To** option to set a time period for when **Night Shift** is applied

5 Tap once on the **Sunset to Sunrise** option to have **Night Shift** applied for this period

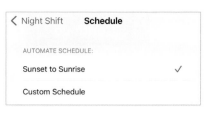

The **Sunset to Sunrise** option is determined by your iPhone's clock and its location as specified by Location Services. Tap on the **Custom Schedule** option in Step 5 to set a specific time period for when **Night Shift** operates.

About Apple Pay

Apple Pay is Apple's service for mobile, contactless payment. It can be used by adding credit, debit, and store cards to your iPhone via the Wallet app, and then paying for items by using your Face ID (or Touch ID for older iPhones) as authorization for payment. Credit, debit, and store cards have to be issued by banks or retailers that support Apple Pay, and there are an increasing number that do so, with more joining on a regular basis. Outlets also have to support Apple Pay but this, too, is increasing and, given the success of the iPhone, is likely to grow at a steady rate.

Setting up Apple Pay

To use Apple Pay, you have to first add your cards to your iPhone (and be signed in to iCloud).

Cards can also be added to the Wallet app at any time from **Settings** > **Wallet & Apple Pay** > **Add Card**.

1 Tap once on the **Wallet** app

2 Tap once on the **Add Credit or Debit Card** link, or tap once on this button

3 Select the type of card to be added and tap once on the **Continue** button

If your bank does not yet support Apple Pay then you will not be able to add your credit or debit card details to the Wallet app.

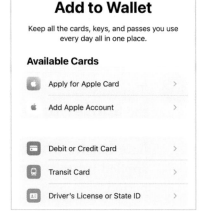

Add to Wallet

Keep all the cards, keys, and passes you use every day all in one place.

Available Cards

	Apply for Apple Card	>
	Add Apple Account	>
	Debit or Credit Card	>
	Transit Card	>
	Driver's License or State ID	>

Continue

4 The card details can be added to the Wallet app by taking a photo of the card. Place the card on a flat surface, and position it within the white box. The card number is then added automatically. Alternatively, tap once on **Enter Card Details Manually**

Add Card

Position your debit or credit card in the frame to scan it.

Enter Card Details Manually

Beware

Obtaining your card number using the camera is not always completely accurate. Take the photo in good light, always check the number afterward, and amend it if necessary.

5 Once the card details have been added, your bank or store card issuer has to verify your card. This can be done either by a text message or a phone call

6 Once the Apple Pay setup process is completed, details of the card appear in the Wallet app

Don't forget

Although no form of contactless payment is 100% secure, Apple Pay does offer some security safeguards. One is that no card information is passed between the retailer and the user; the transaction is done by sending an encrypted token that is used to authorize the payment. Also, the use of the Face ID process ensures another step of authorization that is not available with any other forms of contactless payment.

7 To pay for items with Apple Pay, open the **Wallet** app and tap once on the card you want to use. Hold your iPhone up to the contactless payment card reader. Press the **On/ Off** button twice and look at the phone screen to authorize the payment with Face ID. (Retailers must have a contactless card reader in order for Apple Pay to be used)

Face ID

Using the EarPods

iPhone EarPods are not only an excellent way to listen to music and other audio on your iPhone; they can also be used in a variety of ways with the phone function.

The EarPods contain three main controls:

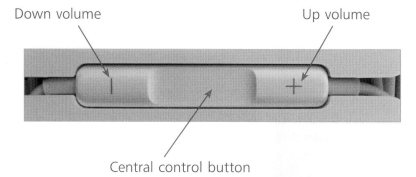

Down volume

Up volume

Central control button

Beware

There are no EarPods provided with the iPhone 14 models. If an existing pair of EarPods is used with an iPhone 14 model, it will need to be one with a Lightning Connector, since the iPhone 14 does not have a separate headphone connection.

64

- Plug in the EarPods to use them to hear someone who is calling you. Speak normally, and the other person will be able to hear you via the EarPods' in-built microphone.

- Click once in the middle of the control button to answer an incoming call.

- Press and hold in the middle of the control button for a couple of seconds (until you hear two beeps) to decline an incoming call.

- Click once in the middle of the control button to end the current call.

- If you are on a call and receive another one, click once in the middle of the control button to put the first call on hold and activate the second call.

- Press and hold in the middle of the control button to dial a number using **Voice Control**, whereby you can speak the required number.

- Click on the control button when playing a music track to pause it. Click again to restart it. Double-click on the control button to move to the next track. Triple-click on the control button to move back to the previous track.

Don't forget

All models of the iPhone 14 can also be used with AirPods, the wireless headphones from Apple.

3 Head in the iCloud

iCloud, the online storage service, is at the heart of the iPhone for backing up your content and sharing it with family and friends.

What is iCloud?

iCloud is the Apple online storage and backup service that performs a number of valuable functions:

- It makes your content available across multiple devices. The content is stored in iCloud and then pushed out to other iCloud-enabled devices, including the iPad and other Mac or Windows computers.

- It enables online access to your content via the iCloud website. This includes your iCloud email, photos, contacts, calendar, reminders, and documents.

- It can back up the content on your iPhone.

To use iCloud you must have an Apple ID. This can be done when you first set up your iPhone, or at a later date. Once you have registered for and set up iCloud, it works automatically so you do not have to worry about anything.

It is free to register for and set up a standard iCloud account.

An Apple ID can be created with an email address and password. It can then be used to access a variety of services, including the iTunes Store, the Book Store, and the App Store.

To access your iCloud account through the website, access **www.icloud.com** and enter your Apple ID details.

1 Tap once on the **Settings** app

2 At the top of the **Settings** panel, tap once on the **Sign in to your iPhone** option

3 If you already have an Apple ID, enter your details and tap once on the **Next** button

4 If you do not yet have an Apple ID, tap once on the **Don't have an Apple ID or forgot it?** link and follow the steps to create your Apple ID

iCloud Settings

Once you have set up your iCloud account, you can then apply settings for how it works. Once you have done this, you will not have to worry about it again.

1 Tap once on the **Apple ID, iCloud, Media & Purchases** section in the Settings app

2 Tap once on the **iCloud** button

3 Tap once on the items in the **Sync With iCloud** section to turn them **On** or **Off**, and apply settings for each item. Tap once on the **Show All** option to view the full range of iCloud-compatible apps

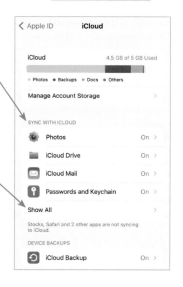

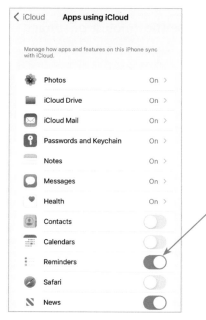

4 Drag these buttons **On** for each item that you wish to be included in iCloud. Each item is then saved and stored in iCloud and made available to your other iCloud-enabled devices

Don't forget

iCloud items can be turned **On** or **Off** at any time, as required. However, it is best to keep most of them activated, unless there is a good reason not to do so.

67

Upgrading to iCloud+

iCloud+ is a paid-for enhancement to iCloud that enables you to add more storage to your iCloud account and also access additional security options. To subscribe to iCloud+:

The default amount of storage for the default iCloud account is 5GB, which is provided free of charge.

1 Tap once on the **iCloud** button as shown in Step 2 on page 67

☁ iCloud   5 GB >

2 The amount of storage that has been used is indicated by the colored bar at the top of the window (e.g. yellow for photos, and blue for email). Tap once on the **Manage Account Storage** option, or

< Apple ID   iCloud

iCloud   4.5 GB of 5 GB Used

● Photos ● Mail ● Docs ● Messages

Manage Account Storage   >

iCloud+ is the equivalent of the iCloud upgrade service from the free version in previous versions of iOS. iCloud+ also has a few additional features – see the next page for details.

3 If the iCloud storage is already full, tap once on the **Upgrade to iCloud+** button to increase the amount of storage

! Your iCloud storage is full
Get iCloud+ to make sure your apps and services keep syncing with iCloud.

Upgrade to iCloud+

4 Select an iCloud+ storage plan

☁ iCloud+   ×

More Storage and Powerful New Features

All iCloud+ plans include Private Relay, Hide My Email, Custom Email Domain, and HomeKit Secure Video.

Learn More About iCloud+

50 GB   £0.79 a month   ✓

200 GB   £2.49 a month   ○

2 TB   £6.99 a month   ○

All plans can be shared with up to five family members. Plan auto-renews for £0.79 / month until canceled.

Upgrade to iCloud+

Not Now

Don't forget

Prices are shown in local currencies.

5 Tap once on the **Upgrade to iCloud+** button

6 Confirmation of the iCloud+ upgrade is displayed. Tap once on the **Done** button

Private Relay
protects your browsing by ensuring that any website interactions are encrypted from your iPhone, and two separate internet relays are used to hide the IP address linked to your iPhone.

7 The iCloud storage is increased, according to the new iCloud+ storage plan

8 Tap once on the **Apple ID** button in the previous step to return to the main Apple ID page

9 Tap once on the **Private Relay** and **Hide My Email** options to use these for internet and email security options

10 For **Private Relay**, drag the **Private Relay** button **On** to protect your browsing activity with Safari

Hide My Email
creates a new, random email address each time you have to enter your email address online, such as for an online retailer, so you never have to enter your own email address.

11 For **Hide My Email**, tap once on the **Create New Address** button to create a random email address that is used to forward messages to your own email account so that people cannot see your email address

69

About Family Sharing

As everyone gets more and more digital devices it is becoming increasingly important to be able to share content with other people, particularly family members. In iOS 16, the **Family Sharing** function enables you to share items that you have downloaded from the Apple stores, such as music and movies, with up to five other family members, as long as they have an Apple ID. Once this has been set up, it is also possible to share items such as family calendars and purchases, and even see where family members are on a map. To set up and start using Family Sharing:

Hot tip

If you create a child account in Step 4 on the next page, you can specify that they have to ask permission before downloading content from the iTunes Store, the App Store or the Book Store. To do this, select them in the **Family Sharing** section and drag the **Ask To Buy** button **On**. For each purchase you will be sent a notification asking for approval.

1 Access the **Apple ID** section within the Settings app, as shown on page 67

2 Tap once on the **Family Sharing** button

3 Details about Family Sharing are displayed. Tap once on the **Continue** button to invite family members or friends to join your Family Sharing group

4 Suggested options are displayed, for inviting people, based on activity within your iPhone apps. Tap once on the **Invite** button to invite a suggested person or tap once on the **Invite Others** button to invite another family member

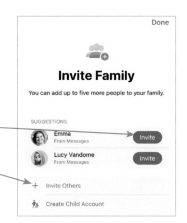

5 Select a method for sending the invitation; e.g. by email

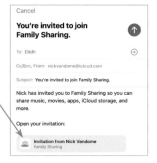

6 An invitation is created automatically (although the text can be edited), with a link in the message that is used by the recipient to activate the invitation. Send the message in the usual way for the selected option

Don't forget

Tap once here to access settings for managing your Family Sharing group.

7 The invited person is added to the **Family** screen (they are not part of the Family Sharing group until they accept the invitation). Tap once on the **Family Checklist** option to view options for the Family Sharing group. Tap once on the **Subscriptions**, **Purchase Sharing** and **Location** options to view details of these items

Using Family Sharing

Once you have set up Family Sharing and added family members, you can start sharing a selection of items.

Sharing subscriptions

There are a number of Apple subscription services, and if you join any of them then you can also share them via Family Sharing. This means that anyone in your Family Sharing group can take advantage of these services too, without having to pay for an additional subscription. The options include:

- **Apple Music**. If a family subscription has been taken out for Apple Music, this can be shared via Family Sharing, providing access to millions of songs.

Apple Music Family Subscription

- **Apple TV+**. This is Apple's subscription service for movies and TV shows. There is a wealth of original content in Apple TV+ that you cannot access elsewhere.

Apple TV+

- **Apple Arcade**. This is a subscription gaming service, with a range of original games that can be played individually, or as multiplayer games with other people.

Apple Arcade

- **iCloud+**. The expanded iCloud service can be made available via Family Sharing, giving access to additional levels of shared storage.

iCloud+

Don't forget

The regular **Apple TV** option can be used to rent or buy movies and TV shows. Both the regular service and **Apple TV+** can be accessed from the **TV** app.

TV

Sharing calendars

Family Sharing also generates a **Family** calendar that can be used by all Family Sharing members.

1. Tap once on the **Calendar** app

2. Tap once on this button and create a new event (see page 163). Select **Family** as the Calendar option to distribute the event to your Family Sharing members

Calendar	● Family ⟳

When someone in the Family Sharing circle adds an event to the **Family** calendar it will appear in your calendar with the appropriate tag. A red notification will also appear on the Calendar app, and it will appear in the Notification Center (if the calendar has been selected to appear here).

Sharing apps, music, books and movies

Family Sharing means that all members of the group can share purchases from the iTunes Store, the App Store or the Book Store, accessed from within the Books app. This is done from the **Purchased** section of each app.

1. Open the relevant app and access the **Purchased** section. (For the **App Store**, tap once on the **Account** icon and tap once on the **Purchased** button; for the **iTunes Store**, tap once on the **Menu** > **Purchased** button on the bottom toolbar; for the **Books** app, tap once on the **Account** icon)

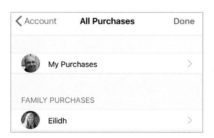

Family Sharing makes it easy to keep in touch with the rest of the family and see exactly where they are. This can be done with the **Find My** app. The other person must have their Apple device turned **On** and be online. To find family members, tap once on the Find My app. The location of any people who are linked via your Family Sharing circle is displayed.

2. For all three apps, tap once on a member under **Family Purchases** to view their purchases and download them, if required, by tapping once on this button

73

iCloud Shared Photo Library

iCloud Shared Photo Library is a new feature in iOS 16.

The **Shared Library** option in Step 2 can also be accessed from **Settings** > **Photos**.

Shared albums can also be set up for the Photos app so that photos and videos can be shared with invited people, from **Settings** > **Photos** > **Shared Albums**. However, unlike a shared library, photos cannot be added directly from the Camera app, and other users cannot edit or delete photos from a shared album.

In addition to Family Sharing, iOS 16 also enables iCloud to create a shared photo library that can then be shared with family and friends. One of the advantages of this is that photos can be shared directly from the Camera app when they are taken. Older photos in the Photos app can also be added to a shared library. To use a shared photo library:

1 Access the **iCloud** section in the Settings app, as shown on page 67, and tap once on the **Photos** option

2 Tap once on the **Shared Library** option

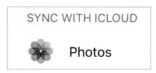

3 In the **Shared Library** section, use these options to apply suggestions and also options for sharing directly from the Camera app

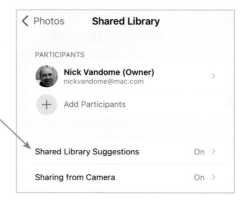

4 Tap once on the **Shared Library Suggestions** option and drag the button **On** to enable photo suggestions from other people who are part of the shared library

5 Tap once on the **Sharing from Camera** option in Step 3 on the previous page to select how photos are added to the shared library when they are taken with the Camera app

6 Tap once on the **Add Participants** option in Step 3 on the previous page to invite people to the shared library

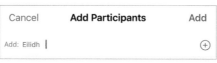

7 Once someone has been invited, this is indicated in the main window. An invitation has to be accepted for someone to join the shared library

8 To add photos to the shared library from the Camera app, tap once on this icon on the top toolbar of the Camera app

9 The icon turns yellow, to indicate that the **Shared Library** feature is activated. Any photos that are taken when this icon is yellow will be added to the shared library

Once someone has joined the shared library they have full access to add photos and videos, and also edit or delete ones that are already in the shared library.

Photos in the Photos app can be added to the shared library. To do this, open them at full size in the Photos app, tap once on the menu button in the top right-hand corner and tap once on the **Move to Shared Library** option.

iCloud Drive and the Files App

One of the features of iCloud is **iCloud Drive**, which can be used to store documents such as those created with the Apple suite of productivity apps (available in the App Store): Pages (word processing), Numbers (spreadsheets), and Keynote (presentations). These documents can then be accessed with the Files app.

Hot tip

The Files app can also be used with other online storage services such as Dropbox and Google Drive, if you have one of these accounts. If so, they will appear under the **Locations** section in Step 3.

Hot tip

Tap once on the **Select** button in Step 4 and tap once on an item to select it. Then, use these buttons to, from left to right: share the selected item; duplicate the item; move the item; or delete the item:

1 Access the **iCloud** settings as shown on page 67 and tap once on the **iCloud Drive** option. Drag the **Sync this iPhone** button **On**

Sync this iPhone

2 Tap once on the **Files** app

3 Tap once on the **iCloud Drive** button to view its contents

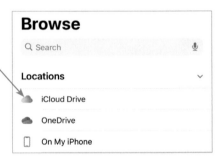

Browse

Q Search

Locations ⌄

☁ iCloud Drive

☁ OneDrive

▢ On My iPhone

4 Tap once on individual folders to view their contents (this will include documents created in their respective apps). Tap once on the **Menu** button and tap once on the **New Folder** button to create a new folder for content

‹ Browse   iCloud Drive   ⋯

Q Search

Annual Membe...p Form   Desktop 0 items   Documents 7 items

iCloud Drive   ⋯

Select   ⊘

New Folder   ▣

4 Calls and Contacts

One of the main uses for the iPhone is still to make and receive phone calls. This chapter shows how to do this and how to manage your contacts.

Adding Contacts

Because of its power and versatility, it is sometimes forgotten that one of the reasons for the iPhone's existence is to make phone calls. Before you start doing this, it is a good idea to add family and friends to the **Contacts** app. This will enable you to phone them without having to tap in their phone number each time. To add a contact:

1 Tap once on the **Contacts** app

2 Any contacts that you already have are displayed

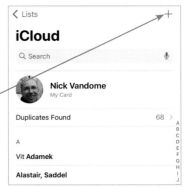

Don't forget

Tap once on the green button next to a box to add another box. Tap once on the red button to delete a box.

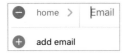

3 Tap once on this button to add a new contact

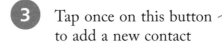

4 Enter a name for the contact at the top of the window, in the **First name** and **Last name** boxes

Don't forget

Tap once on the **Add Photo** option in Step 4 to add a photo for a new contact from your Photos Library or by taking one with the camera.

5 Tap once in one of the Phone boxes, or tap once on the **add phone** button to add a new Phone box

6 Enter the required number with the number pad that is activated when you tap in a Phone box

7 Tap once on the **Done** button to add the new contact

8 The contact is added under **Contacts**

9 Tap once on a contact to view their full details. You can use these buttons at the top of the window to: send them a text; make a voice call to them; make a video call; send them an email (if their email address is included); or send them money via Apple Pay (if this is available)

Use the buttons at the bottom of a contact's window to send them a message, share their details with other people, add them as a favorite or share your location with them. If someone is added as a favorite, they can be accessed directly from the **Favorites** button on the bottom toolbar of the **Phone** app.

Making a Call

The iPhone can be used to make calls to specific phone numbers that you enter manually, or to contacts in your Contacts app.

Dialing a number

To make a call by dialing a specific number, first tap once on the **Phone** app.

80

1 Tap once on the **Keypad** button at the bottom of the window

2 Tap on the numbers on the keypad to enter the number, which appears at the top of the window. Tap on this button to delete a number that has been entered

3 Tap once on this button to make the call

Calling a contact

To call someone who has been added to the Contacts app:

1 Open the **Phone** app, and tap once on the **Contacts** button at the bottom of the window. The Contacts app opens, with the Phone toolbar still visible at the bottom of the window

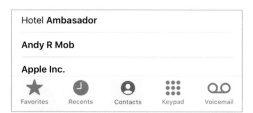

2 Tap once on a contact

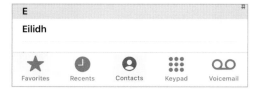

3 Full details for the contact are displayed. Tap once on the **mobile** button at the top of the window to call the number of the contact (the button can display **call** in some instances)

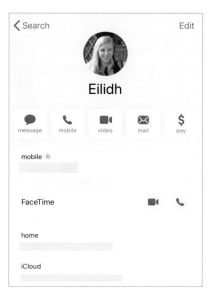

Hot tip

To find someone in the Contacts app (either directly from the app or from the **Contacts** button in the Phone app), swipe up and down on the screen; enter a name in the Search box at the top of the window; or tap on a letter on the alphabetic list down the right-hand side.

81

Don't forget

The banner in Step 1 is known as a Compact Call.

Don't forget

When a call is connected, tap on the banner and the following buttons appear on the screen. Use them to: mute a call; access the keypad again, in case you need to add any more information such as for an automated call; access the speaker so that you do not have to keep the phone at your ear; add another call to create a conference call; make a FaceTime call to the caller (if they have this facility); or access your Contacts app.

Receiving a Call

When you receive a call, there are two main options.

Calls when the iPhone is unlocked

1 When you receive a call, the person's name and photo (if they have been added to your contacts) or number appears in a banner at the top of the screen

2 Tap once on this button to accept the call. Initially, the screen will display options for **Remind Me** and **Message** (see the next page). Tap once on this button to connect the call

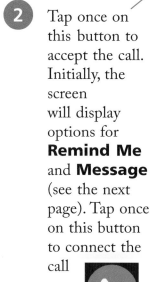

3 Tap once on this button to decline the call

…cont'd

Calls when the iPhone is locked

If you receive a call while your iPhone is locked, it will be displayed on the Lock screen. If this happens, there are various options on the Lock screen in terms of what can be done with the call.

1 Swipe this button from left to right to answer the call

The reminder in Step 3 will appear on the Lock screen at the specified time.

2 Tap once on the **Remind Me** button to decline the call but set a reminder

3 Tap once on one of the options for when you are reminded about the call. The options are **In 1 hour** or **When I leave** (if Location Services is turned **On** in **Settings** > **Privacy & Security**)

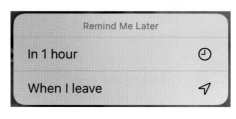

4 Tap once on the **Message** button to decline the call but send the person a text message instead

Tap once on the **Custom...** button in Step 5 to create your own customized text message to send to the caller.

5 Tap once on the text message that you want to send

Saving Phone Contacts

Another quick way to add a contact is to ask someone to phone you so that you can then copy their number directly from your phone to your contacts. You do not even have to answer the phone to do this.

Hot tip

Information from a caller can also be added to an existing contact. For instance, if one of your contacts calls you from a different phone, these details can be added to their existing information. To do this, tap once on the **Add to Existing Contact** button in Step 5.

1 Once someone has phoned, tap once on the **Phone** app

2 Tap once on the **Recents** button at the bottom of the window

3 The call will be displayed. Tap once on the **i** symbol

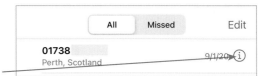

4 Information about the call is displayed, including the number

5 Tap once on the **Create New Contact** button

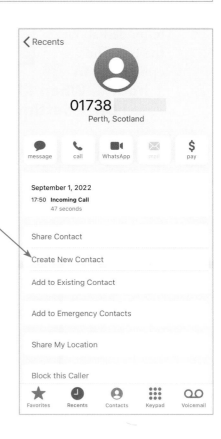

Hot tip

To block a number from contacting you, tap once on the **Block this Caller** button in Step 5.

Block this Caller

6 A **New Contact** window opens, with the number already preinserted

If a photo is not added for a contact using the **Add Photo** button in Step 6, the contact's initials will be displayed at the top of the window.

7 Add information for the contact as required, such as name, any additional phone numbers, and email

8 Tap once on the **Done** button to add the new contact

Merging duplicate entries in the Contacts app is a new feature in iOS 16.

Merging Duplicate Contacts

In previous versions of iOS, one of the idiosyncrasies of the operating system was that it was prone to creating a large number of duplicate entries in the Contacts app. This was partly due to it being linked to the iCloud function, which resulted in a large number of duplicate entries there and on an iPhone, even several entries for the same person, which could be annoying and confusing. Thankfully, this has been resolved in iOS 16, with an option to merge contacts. To do this:

1 Tap once on the **Contacts** app

2 If there are duplicates within the Contacts app, tap once on the **Duplicates Found** option

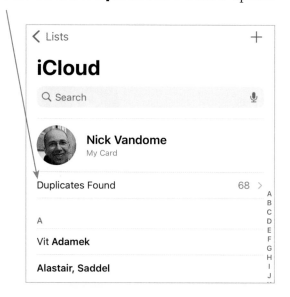

3 Tap once on the **Merge All** button

4 Tap once on the **Merge Duplicates** button to confirm the action

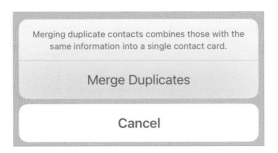

Merging duplicate contacts combines those with the same information into a single contact card.

Merge Duplicates

Cancel

Don't forget

5 If the action is successful, the **Duplicates Resolved** title is displayed

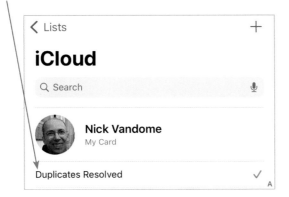

‹ Lists   +

iCloud

Q Search   🎤

Nick Vandome
My Card

Duplicates Resolved   ✓
                    A

If duplicate entries in the Contacts app are merged on your iPhone, the action will be performed for contacts on all of your Apple devices, as long as they are all linked to the same Apple ID.

6 If more duplicates are generated in the future, tap once on the **Duplicates Found** option again to repeat the process

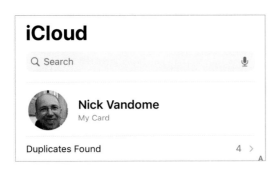

iCloud

Q Search   🎤

Nick Vandome
My Card

Duplicates Found   4 ›
                    A

Hot tip

Tap once on the **Tone Store** button in the **Ringtone** window to go to the iTunes Store, where you can download more ringtones, from the **Tones** button.

Tone Store

Don't forget

If the **Ringer** button on the side of the iPhone (see page 12) is turned **Off**, the iPhone can still be set to vibrate if a call or notification is received, using the **Play Haptics in Silent Mode** button in the main **Sounds & Haptics** window (drag the button **On**).

Setting Ringtones

Ringtones were one of the original "killer apps" for mobile/cell phones: a must-have accessory that helped transform the way people looked at these devices. The iPhone has a range of ringtones that can be used, and you can also download and install thousands more. To use the default ringtones:

1 Tap once on the **Settings** app

2 Tap once on the **Sounds & Haptics** tab

3 Tap once on the **Ringtone**
link under **Sounds and Haptic Patterns** to select ringtones for when you receive a phone call

4 Tap once on one of the options to hear a preview and select it

5 Sounds and vibrations can also be selected for a range of other items such as text messages, email, and calendar and reminder alerts, by going back to the **Sounds and Haptic Patterns** section and choosing a tone for each item

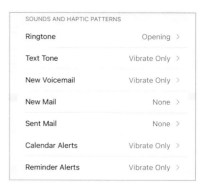

Adding individual ringtones

It is also possible to set ringtones for individual people so that you know immediately who a call is from.

1 Select a contact in the Contacts app, and tap on the **Edit** button

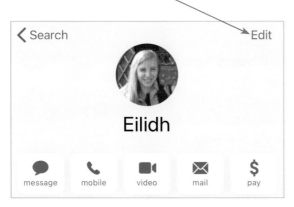

Only set ringtones for your most regular contacts, otherwise you may end up with too many variations.

2 Tap once on the **Ringtone** button

If you are going to be using your iPhone around other people, consider turning the **Keyboard Feedback** options (toward the bottom of the main **Sounds & Haptics** settings window) **Off**, as the noise can get annoying for those in the vicinity. The options are for **Sound** and **Haptic**, both of which can be turned **Off**.

3 Tap once on a ringtone to assign this to the contact

RINGTONES

Bulletin

Apex

Beacon

✓ By The Seaside

Chimes

Phone Settings

As with most of the iPhone functions, there are a range of settings for the phone itself. To use them:

Don't forget

Use the options for **Cellular** (**Mobile**) settings for items specific to your phone service provider.

1 Tap once on the **Settings** app

2 Tap once on the **Phone** tab

3 The **Phone** settings have options for responding with a text message to a call that you do not take (see the next step); call forwarding; call waiting; and silencing the phone's ringer when it receives an unknown number (see the Hot tip)

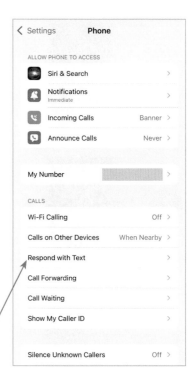

Hot tip

Drag the **Silence Unknown Callers** button **On** in Step 3 to ensure that any calls from numbers that you do not recognize (those not in your contacts) are silenced; i.e. the phone will not ring.

4 Tap once on the **Respond with Text** button to create a text message that can be sent if you do not want to answer a call when it is received

5 Typing and Texts

This chapter shows how to use the iPhone keyboard to add text, and also shows the range of items that can be added to messages with iOS 16. It also covers Shared with You, for viewing items other people send you.

The iPhone Keyboard

The keyboard on the iPhone is a virtual one; i.e. it appears on the touchscreen whenever text or numbered input is required for an app. This can be for a variety of reasons:

- Entering text with a word processing app, or into an email or an organizing app such as Notes.

- Entering a web address in a web browser such as the Safari app.

- Entering information into an online form.

- Entering a password.

Viewing the keyboard

When you attempt one of the actions above, the keyboard appears so that you can enter any text or numbers.

Space bar

Shift button

Around the keyboard

To access the various keyboard controls:

1 Tap once on the **Shift** button to create a **Cap** (capital) text letter

2 Double-tap on the **Shift** button to enable **Caps Lock**

3 Tap once on this button to back-delete an item

Hot tip

In some apps such as Notes, Mail and Messages, it is possible to change the keyboard into a trackpad for moving the cursor. To do this, press and hold firmly on the keyboard, and then swipe over the trackpad to move the cursor around.

Hot tip

It is possible to increase the size of view of the iPhone keyboard with the **Zoom** feature within the **Accessibility** settings – see pages 178-179 for details.

Don't forget

To return from Caps Lock, tap once on the **Caps** button.

4 Tap once on this button to access the **Numbers** keyboard option

93

5 From the **Numbers** keyboard, tap once on this button to access the **Symbols** keyboard

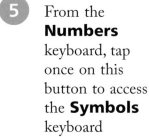

Hot tip

If you are entering a password, or details into a form, the keyboard will have a **Go** or **Send** button that can be used to activate the information that has been entered.

6 Tap once on this button on either of the two keyboards above to return to the standard QWERTY option

Shortcut keys

Instead of having to go to a different keyboard every time you want to add punctuation (or numbers), there is a shortcut for this.

Hot tip

Several keys have additional options that can be accessed by pressing and holding on the key. A lot of these are letters that have accented versions in different languages; e.g. a, e, i, o and u. Swipe across a letter to add it.

1 Press and hold on the **Numbers** button, and swipe over the item you want to include. This will be added, and you will remain on the QWERTY keyboard

Keyboard Settings

Settings for the keyboard can be determined in the **General** section of the Settings app. To do this:

Drag the **Predictive** button **On** to enable predictive texting (see pages 96-97). Drag the **Character Preview** button **On** to show a magnified example of a letter or symbol when it is pressed, to ensure that the correct one is selected.

The **Auto-Correction** function works as you type a word, so it may change a number of times depending on the length of the word you are typing.

1 Tap once on the **Settings** app

2 Tap once on the **General** tab

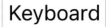

3 Tap once on the **Keyboard** link

Keyboard

4 Drag the **Auto-Capitalization** button **On** to automatically capitalize letters at the beginning of a sentence

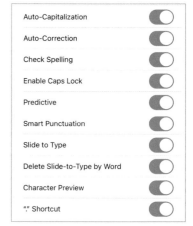

5 Drag the **Auto-Correction** button **On** to enable suggestions for words to appear as you type, particularly if you have mistyped a word

6 Drag the **Check Spelling** and **Smart Punctuation** buttons **On** to identify misspelled words and add punctuation

7 Drag the **Enable Caps Lock** button **On** to enable this function to be performed

8 Drag the **"." Shortcut** button **On** to add a period (full stop) and a space to start a new sentence by just tapping the space bar twice

9 Tap once on the **Text Replacement** option to view existing text shortcuts and create new ones

10 Tap once on this button to create new shortcuts

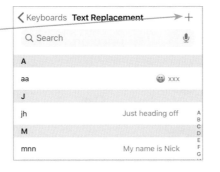

Third-party keyboards can be downloaded from the App Store and used instead of the default one. One to look at is Grammarly.

11 Enter a phrase and the shortcut you want to use to create it when you type. Tap once on the **Save** button

12 Tap once on the **Keyboards** button in Step 9 to add a new keyboard

13 Tap once on the **Add New Keyboard...** button

Add New Keyboard...

14 Tap once on a keyboard to add it. The keyboard will be available by selecting the globe icon (see the Don't forget tip)

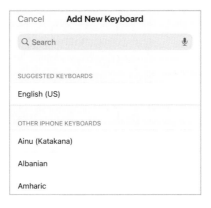

By default, two keyboards are installed: one for the language of your region, and the emoji one. If more keyboards are added, this symbol will appear below the keyboard. Press on it to select another keyboard from the one being used.

95

Using Predictive Text

Predictive text tries to guess what you are typing, and also predicts the next word following the one you have just typed. It is excellent for text messaging. To use it:

1 Tap once on the **General** tab in the Settings app

2 Tap once on the **Keyboard** link

3 Drag the **Predictive** button **On**

4 When predictive text is being used, the QuickType bar is displayed above the keyboard.

Initially, before you start a new message, the QuickType bar is not visible; it only become available when you start typing in the text box

5 As you type, suggestions appear. Tap on one to accept it. Tap once on the word within quotation marks to accept exactly what you have typed

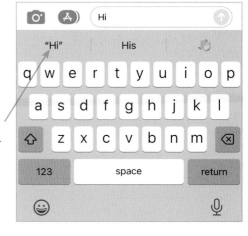

Don't forget

Predictive text learns from your writing style as you write, and so gets more accurate at predicting words. It can also recognize a change in style for different apps such as Mail and Messages.

6 If you continue typing, the predictive suggestions will change as you add more letters

7 After you have typed a word, a suggestion for the next word appears. Tap on one of the suggestions or start typing a new word, which will then also have predictive suggestions as you type

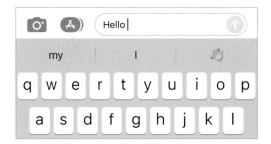

Toggling predictive text from the keyboard

You can also toggle predictive text **On** or **Off** from the keyboard. To do this:

1 Press and hold on this button on the keyboard

2 Tap once on the **Keyboard Settings...** button to access the **Predictive** setting, from where it can be turned **On** or **Off**

Hot tip

It is also possible to create text by swiping over letters on the keyboard. This is known as QuickPath typing. To set this up, access **Settings > General > Keyboard** and turn **Slide to Type** On.

Text can then be created by sliding your fingers over the required letters, rather than tapping on them individually.

Hot tip

Tapping the button in Step 1 allows you to add emojis, which are symbols used in text messages to signify happiness, surprise, sadness, etc. (See page 104 for details.)

One-Handed Keyboard

When typing with the iPhone, this is frequently done with one hand. To make this easier, there is an option for formatting the keyboard for one-handed typing. To do this:

1 Open the **General** tab in the Settings app and tap on **Keyboard**, then tap once on the **One-Handed Keyboard** link

2 Select the **Left** or **Right** option for the keyboard

Beware

When using your iPhone one-handed, make sure you keep a good hold on it so that it does not fall on the ground.

3 If more than one keyboard has been added (e.g. the emoji keyboard), press and hold on this button on the keyboard, and tap once on the options for moving the keyboard to the left or right

4 The keyboard is moved into the position selected in either Step 2 or 3. Tap once here to revert to the original keyboard

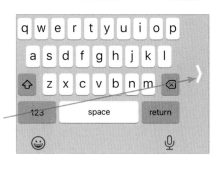

Entering Text

Once you have applied the keyboard settings that you require, you can start entering text. To do this:

1 Tap once on the screen to activate the keyboard from the app. Start typing with the keyboard. The text will appear at the point where you tapped on the screen

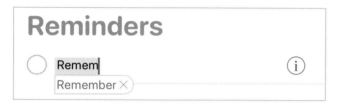

2 As you type, Auto-Correction comes up with suggestions (if it is turned **On**). Tap once on the space bar to accept the suggestion, or tap once on the cross next to it to reject it

3 If **Check Spelling** is enabled in the keyboard settings, any misspelled words appear highlighted. Press on the word to access a replacement word. Tap once on the replacement to use it, if required

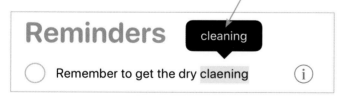

4 Double-tap the space bar to enter a period (full stop) and a space at the end of a sentence

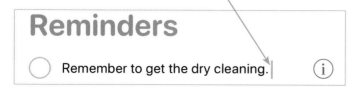

If you keep typing as normal, the **Auto-Correction** suggestion will disappear when you finish the word.

If predictive text is turned **On** (**Settings > General > Keyboard > Predictive**), the **Auto-Correction** suggestions will appear on the QuickType bar above the keyboard, rather than below the word being typed, as in Step 1.

The **"."** **Shortcut** option has to be turned **On** (**Settings > General > Keyboard > "." Shortcut**) for the functionality in Step 4 to work (see Step 8 on page 94).

Editing Text

Once text has been entered it can be selected, copied, cut, and pasted. Depending on the app being used, the text can also be formatted, such as with a word processing app.

Managing text

To work with text in a document you have created:

1 To change the insertion point in a document, press on the cursor to pick it up

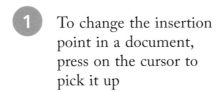

Moving the cursor.

2 Drag the cursor to move the insertion point

Moving the cursor.

3 Tap once at the insertion point to access the menu buttons

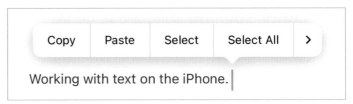

| Copy | Paste | Select | Select All | > |

Working with text on the iPhone.

4 Double-tap on a word to select it. Tap once on one of the menu buttons, as required

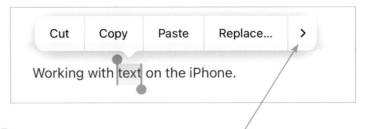

| Cut | Copy | Paste | Replace... | > |

Working with text on the iPhone.

5 Tap once on this button to access more options for working with the selected text (see the second Hot tip)

Selecting text

Text can be selected using a range of methods.

1 Double-tap on a word to select it

2 Drag the selection handles to increase or decrease the selection. This is a good way to select certain text within a sentence or within a paragraph

3 Triple-tap on a word to select the whole of its related paragraph

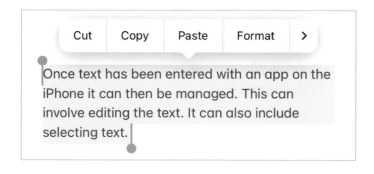

Hot tip

You can also add someone from your contacts by typing their name into the **To:** box shown in Step 3. As you start typing, names will appear for you to select from. You can type the telephone number of anyone who isn't in your contacts here, too.

Hot tip

You can also send family and friends audio clips in an iMessage so that they can hear from you too. To do this, tap on the microphone icon at the right-hand side of the text box, or on the keyboard, and record your message.

Text Messaging

Text messages sent with the Messages app can either be iMessages or SMS text messages, depending on how they are sent. iMessages are sent using Wi-Fi to other users with an Apple ID and using an iPhone, iPad, or a Mac computer. SMS text messages are just sent via your cellular (mobile) carrier. When you send an iMessage, it appears in a blue bubble in the Messages app; when you send an SMS text, it appears in a green bubble.

1 Tap once on the **Messages** app

2 Tap once on this button to create a new message and start a new conversation

3 Tap once on this button to select someone from your contacts

New iMessage	Cancel
To:	⊕

4 Tap once on a contact to select them as the recipient of the new message

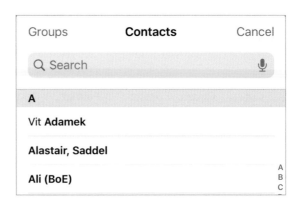

5 Tap once here, and type with the keyboard to create a message

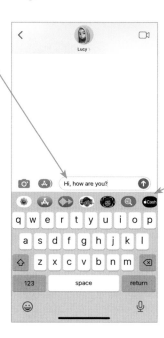

6 Tap once on this button to send a message (it is not available until a message has been composed)

7 As the conversation progresses, each message is displayed in the main window

The App Strip, containing options for adding content to a text message, is available below the text box. Tap once on this button to show or hide the App Strip:

When a message has been sent, you are notified underneath it when it has been delivered.

Money can be transferred to other people by tapping on this button on the App Strip:

Cash

To use this service, Apple Pay and Apple Pay Cash have to be set up on your own iPhone and the recipient's.

Enhancing Text Messages

Adding emojis

Emojis (small graphical symbols) are very popular in text messages, and there is now a huge range in iOS 16. To add these:

1 Tap once on this button on the keyboard to view the emoji keyboards

2 Swipe left and right to view the emoji options. Tap once on an emoji to add it to a message

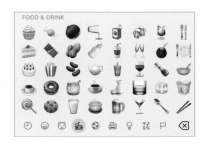

Emojis can be added automatically from certain words.

1 Add text, and tap once on the button in Step 1 above. Items that can be replaced are highlighted

I like to eat cake on a train

I like to eat cake on a train

2 Tap once on a highlighted word to see the emoji options. Tap once on one to add it to the message

I like to eat cake on a train

Full-screen messages

iMessages can also be sent with full-screen effects.

1 Write a message, and press and hold on this button

2 Tap once on the **Screen** button at the top of the window

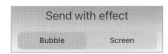

3 Different animated options can be selected to accompany the message

4 Swipe to the left, or tap on these buttons to view different animated effects

Bubble messages

A range of other effects can also be added to text messages.

1 Tap once on the button in Step 1 for full-screen messages above and tap once on the **Bubble** button to create a message with one of the following effects: **Slam**; **Loud**; **Gentle**; or **Invisible Ink**

Hot tip

Memojis are animated stickers that can take on the expressions and voice of the person looking at the iPhone's camera. To add a Memoji to a text message, tap once on this icon below the text box,  select the required icon and tap once on the record button to create a Memoji.

Hot tip

Once a **Screen** or **Bubble** effect has been added, tap once on this button to send the message:

Editing and Unsending iMessages

Editing and unsending text messages is a new feature in iOS 16.

Don't forget

iMessages can be edited up to five times within 15 minutes of them being sent. They can be unsent within two minutes of being sent.

Beware

Editing and unsending iMessages is only effective if they are sent to other people using iOS 16 (or iPadOS 16 for an iPad and macOS Ventura for a Mac computer). If not, the editing and unsending operations may not work and the recipient will just see the original message.

When sending text iMessages from an iPhone using iOS 16 it is now possible to edit messages with any typos or mistakes in them, and also unsend a message if it has been sent in error or contains something that you didn't mean to include, although there is a time limit for these operations.

Editing an iMessage

1 Press and hold on a message once it has been sent and tap once on the **Edit** button

> Just testing something - ignore this!
> Delivered

Edit

2 Edit the message as required and tap once on this icon (the check mark symbol)

> Just testing something! ✓
> Delivered

3 The edited text is displayed in the conversation window

> Just testing something!
> Delivered · Edited

Unsending an iMessage

1 Press and hold on a message once it has been sent and tap once on the **Undo Send** button

Undo Send

2 A message is displayed to indicate that the message has been unsent

> Today 15:33
> You unsent a message. Lucy may still see the message on devices where the software hasn't been updated.

Voice Typing

On the keyboard there is also a voice-typing option that enables you to enter text by speaking into a microphone, rather than typing on the keyboard. This is **On** by default.

Using voice typing

Voice typing (dictation) can be used with any app with a text input function. To do this:

1 Press and hold on this button on the keyboard to activate the voice-typing microphone. Speak into the microphone to record text

2 As you speak into the microphone, text appears in the app you're using, with this icon, indicating that voice typing is being used. Tap on it once to disable voice typing

Voice typing is not an exact science, and you may find that some strange examples appear. The best results are created if you speak as clearly as possible and reasonably slowly.

Hot tip

Dictation can be turned **On** or **Off** in **Settings** > **General** > **Keyboard** > **Enable Dictation**.

Don't forget

There are other voice-typing apps available from the App Store. One to try is Dragon Anywhere.

Settings for the Messages app can be applied in the Settings app.

Press and hold on a message that you have received, and tap once on one of these icons to send it as a reply:

This is known as Tapback.

Whole conversations can be deleted, by swiping from right to left on them in the main **Messages** window and tapping once on this icon:

Managing Messages

Text conversations with individuals can become quite lengthy, so it is sometimes a good idea to remove some messages while still keeping the conversation going.

1 As a conversation with one person progresses, it moves downward in the window

2 Press and hold on a message that you want to delete, and tap once on the **More...** button

3 Tap once next to any message that you want to delete, so that a white check mark in a blue circle appears

4 Tap once on the **Trash** icon to delete the selected message(s)

6 Camera and Photos

The iPhone has a high-quality camera, and the Photos app for viewing your photos.

The iPhone cameras have been updated with the iPhone 14.

To take a quick photo, open the **Camera** app and press on either of the **Volume** buttons on the side of the iPhone.

Whenever you access your iPhone's camera, a small green dot appears at the top of the screen to indicate that the camera is in operation. This is a security feature so that you can see if anything has accessed your camera when you did not expect it.

The iPhone Camera

The cameras on the iPhone 14 range have the highest specifications to be included with any iPhone, and they take the art of digital photography on a smartphone to a new level. The iPhone 14 Pro and Pro Max are particularly effective for photos as they include three separate lenses, to enable a far greater area to be included in photos.

iPhone 14 camera

The main iPhone 14 and iPhone 14 Plus cameras consist of two lenses.

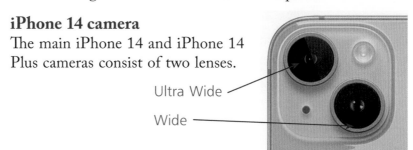

Ultra Wide

Wide

Tap on these buttons on the camera screen to switch between the two lenses:

iPhone 14 Pro and Pro Max camera

The camera on the iPhone 14 Pro and Pro Max consists of three lenses.

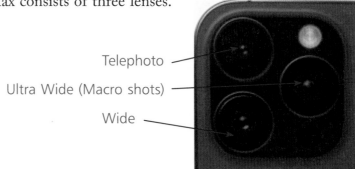

Telephoto

Ultra Wide (Macro shots)

Wide

Some of the features of the iPhone 14 cameras are:

- LiDAR scanners on the Pro models for improved photos in low-level lighting.

- Portrait mode on all models.

- Photographic styles on all models.

- Cinematic mode for video on all models.

...cont'd

Camera functionality

The general functionality of the iPhone 14 cameras can be accessed within the Camera app.

1 Tap once on the **Camera** app

2 Swipe here and select the **Photo** option. Tap once on this button to capture a photo

PHOTO   PORTRAIT

3 Tap once on this button to swap between the front and back cameras on the iPhone

Swipe left or right just above the shutter button, to access the different shooting options.

1 Tap once on the **Video** button and press the red shutter button to take a video

SLO-MO   VIDEO   PHOTO

2 Tap once on the **Time-Lapse** button and press the shutter button (which appears in red with a ring around it) to create a time-lapse image: the camera keeps taking photos periodically until you press the shutter button again

TIME-LAPSE   SLO-MO

Hot tip

Videos can also be captured from the **Photo** option. To do this, press and hold on the shutter button until it turns into the **Video** button. A video should start recording automatically. Release the button to end a video capture. When any video is captured it is stored within the **Photos** app.

Hot tip

Use the front-facing TrueDepth camera to take selfies (self-portraits of yourself, or a group of people). Use the **Slo-Mo** button to take a slow-motion video selfie, which Apple has decided to call a "slowfie".

...cont'd

Tap once on this button on the top toolbar to turn it yellow, to take a Live Photo. This is a short, animated image that can be viewed and edited in the Photos app.

3 Tap once on the **Slo-Mo** button and press the red shutter button to take a slow-motion video

4 Tap once on the **Pano** button to create a panoramic image

5 Move the iPhone slowly to the right to create a panorama. Each photo will be taken automatically when the camera is in the correct position

Camera functions

There are several options in the main camera window.

Tap once on this button on the bottom toolbar to apply a filter effect:
When a filter effect has been selected, this button is displayed in the top right-hand corner of the camera window. It remains active until it is turned Off. To do this, tap once on the button to access the filters, and tap once on **Original**.

1 Tap once on the **Flash** button to set it for **Auto**, **On** or **Off.** Tap once on the **HDR** button, so it does not have a line through it, to take a composite photo of three separate images, to achieve the best exposure

2 Tap once on this button to expand the toolbar (which then appears at the bottom of the camera window). Select options for, from left to right: the **Flash**; **Live Photos** (see the top Don't forget tip); the **Aspect** (shape) of the photo; the **Self-timer** option; **Filters** (see the second Don't forget tip); and **HDR**

Portrait mode

Taking photos of people is one of the most common uses for the iPhone's camera. Using the iPhone camera in **Portrait** mode, it is possible to change the lighting of the photo. To do this:

1 Swipe here and tap once on the **Portrait** button to access options for portrait shots

2 The lighting options are shown above the **Portrait** button. Tap once on each option to select the required lighting mode

Adding depth of field

Portrait photos can be enhanced by blurring the background behind the subject so that they are more prominent. This is known as "depth of field". To do this:

1 Open the **Photos** app, tap once on a photo taken in Portrait mode and tap once on the **Edit** button

2 Tap once on the **f** number icon in the top left-hand corner, and drag this slider to apply a blurred effect to the background of the photo. The main subject will remain unchanged

3 Tap once on the **Done** button to apply a depth-of-field effect to the photo

Hot tip

When creating a depth-of-field effect, ensure the **Portrait** button at the top of the Edit screen is **On**; e.g. yellow. Tap on it once to turn it **Off** and edit the whole photo, not just the background.

⬡ PORTRAIT

Photo Settings

iCloud sharing

Certain photo options can be applied within Settings. Several of these are to do with storing and sharing your photos via iCloud. To access these:

1 Tap once on the **Settings** app

2 Tap once on the **Photos** tab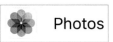

3 Drag the **iCloud Photos** button

On to upload your whole iPhone Photos Library to iCloud. You will then be able to access this from any other Apple devices that you have. Similarly, photos on your other Apple devices can also be uploaded to iCloud, and these will be available on your iPhone

4 Drag the **Shared Albums** button **On**

to allow you to create albums within the Photos app that can then be shared with other people via iCloud

5 Tap once on the **Optimize iPhone Storage** option to save photos on your iPhone at a reduced size, to save storage space (the photos will still be stored at full size in iCloud)

Viewing Photos

Once photos have been captured, they can be viewed and organized in the Photos app. To do this:

1 Tap once on the **Photos** app

2 Tap once on the **Library** button on the bottom toolbar to view photos according to when they were taken, by **Years**, **Months**, **Days**, or **All Photos**

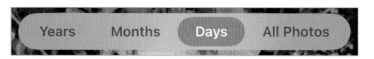

3 Photos are displayed according to the category selected in Step 2

4 If photos are displayed in **Days** or **All Photos** mode, tap once on the **Select** button to select specific photos by tapping on them, or by dragging over several photos

Select

5 Once photos have been selected, or if they are being viewed at full size, tap once on this button to **Share** them

For You Tab

In the Photos app, the **For You** section is where the best of your photos are selected and displayed automatically. To use this:

1 Tap once on the **For You** button on the bottom toolbar of the Photos app

2 Memories are displayed in the **For You** section. These are collections of photos created by the Photos app, using what it determines are the best shots for a related series of photos

When a Memory is playing, as shown in Step 3, tap once on this menu button in the top right-hand corner of the screen to access options for editing the slideshow, including editing the photos used, and editing the title and the speed of the slideshow:

Tap once on this button in the bottom left-hand corner to change the music and effects for the slideshow:

3 Tap once on a Memory to play it as a full-screen slideshow, with music. Tap once on this button to pause, or play, the slideshow

4 Swipe down the **For You** page to access more options for how photos are grouped and organized

Editing Photos

The Photos app has options to perform a range of photo-editing operations. To use these:

1 Open a photo at full-screen size and tap once on the **Edit** button to access the editing tools, on the bottom toolbar

2 Tap once on the **Adjust** button to access color-editing options

3 Tap once on the **Auto** button to have auto-coloring editing applied to the photo

4 Swipe from right to left to access the full range of **Adjust** options

5 For each option, drag the slider to apply the required level of effect

Beware

Editing changes are made to the original photo once the changes have been saved. These will also apply to any albums into which the photo has been placed.

Don't forget

The **Adjust** color-editing options include: Exposure; Brilliance; Highlights; Shadows; Contrast; Brightness; Saturation; and Vibrance.

Hot tip

Videos can also have the same range of editing effects applied to them as still photos.

...cont'd

6 Tap once on the **Filters** button in Step 1 on page 117 to select special effects to be applied to the photo. Swipe left and right here to view the available filters. Tap once on one to apply it

118

7 Tap once on this button in Step 1 on page 117 to access options for rotating the photo and cropping it, by dragging the resizing handles around the border of the photo. Use these options to, from left to right: straighten the photo by dragging the slider; flip it vertically; and flip it horizontally

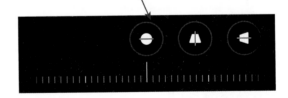

Check out Smartphone Photography in easy steps and 100 Top Tips – Create Great Photos Using Your Smartphone at www. ineasysteps.com for more on using your iPhone to create stunning photographs.

8 For each function, tap once on the **Done** button to save the photo with the selected changes

9 Tap once on the **Cancel** button to quit the editing process

7 The Online World

This chapter shows how to use your iPhone to keep ahead in the fast-moving world of online communications, using the web, email, social media, and video calls.

You can also get online access through your cellular/mobile network, which is provided by your phone network supplier. However, data charges may apply for this.

If you are connecting to your home Wi-Fi network, the iPhone should connect automatically each time after it has been set up. If you are connecting in a public Wi-Fi area, you will be asked which network you would like to join.

Getting Online

Connecting to Wi-Fi is one of the main ways that the iPhone can get online access. You will need to have an Internet Service Provider (ISP) and a Wi-Fi router to connect to the internet. Once this is in place, you will be able to connect to a Wi-Fi network.

1 Tap once on the **Settings** app

2 Tap once on the **Wi-Fi** tab

3 Ensure the **Wi-Fi** button is in the **On** position

4 Available networks are shown here. Tap once on one to select it

5 Enter the password for your Wi-Fi router

6 Tap once on the **Join** button

7 Once a network has been joined, a check mark appears next to it. This now provides access to the internet

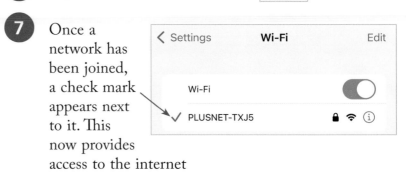

Safari Settings

Safari is the default web browser on the iPhone, and it can be used to bring the web to your iPhone. Before you start using Safari, there are a range of settings that can be applied.

1 Tap once on the **Settings** app

2 Tap once on the **Safari** tab

3 Make selections under the **Search** section for the default search engine, options for suggestions appearing as you type search words and phrases, and preloading the top-rating page in a search

4 Make selections under the **General** section for entering passwords, specifying the items for the **Favorites** window, and blocking pop-ups

5 Make selections under the **Privacy & Security** section for blocking cookies, warning about fraudulent websites, checking to see whether websites accept Apple Pay, and clearing your web browsing history and web data

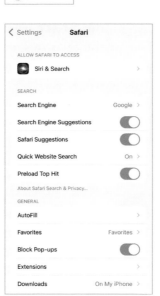

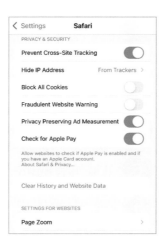

Because of the proliferation of apps available for the iPhone, you may find that you use Safari less than on a desktop or laptop computer. For example, most major news outlets have their own apps that can be used as stand-alone items, rather than having to use Safari to access the site. Look for apps for your favorite websites in the App Store, as a shortcut for accessing them quickly.

The location of the Search/Address bar (see page 122) can be changed in **Settings > Safari** by selecting **Tab Bar** to position the box at the bottom of the screen. Select **Single Tab** to position it at the top of the screen.

Web Browsing with Safari

To start browsing the web with Safari and enjoy the variety of the information within it:

Hot tip

Tap once on this button in the Address Bar to access the web page options, including: **Show Reader**, for viewing pages without additional content; translation options; **Hide Toolbar**; **Request Desktop Website**; **Website Settings**; a **Privacy Report** that shows any websites that are tracking your online activity; and **Show Bottom Tab Bar**, to show a list of open tabs at the bottom of the screen rather than the top.

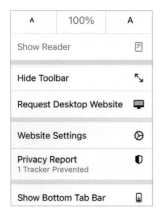

1   Tap once on the **Safari** app

2   Enter a website address here — in the Address Bar, or tap once on one of the items in the **Start** page – e.g. one of the favorites, or one of the Siri suggestions

3   As you type in the Address Bar, website suggestions appear, and also search suggestions from Google (or whichever search engine you selected in Step 3 on page 121)

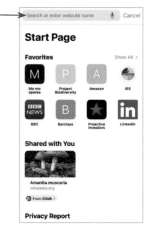

4   When you access a web page, use these buttons to visit the next and previous pages

5   Use this button to share a web page

6   Use this button to view bookmarks

7   Use this button to view, add and delete tabs (see pages 124-125)

Adding bookmarks

Everyone has favorite websites that they visit, and in Safari it is possible to mark these with bookmarks so that they can be accessed quickly. To do this:

1 Tap once on this button on the bottom toolbar

2 Tap once on the **Add Bookmark** button

3 Select a name and location for the bookmark, and tap once on the **Save** button

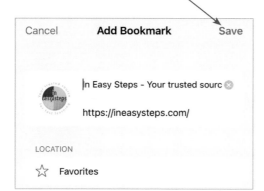

4 Tap once on the **Bookmarks** button, and tap once here to view your bookmarks

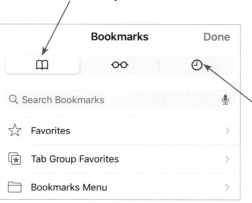

The **Share** button can be used to share a web page via Messages, Mail, or social media sites such as Facebook or Twitter.

If the bottom toolbar is not visible on a web page, swipe downward on the page to view it.

123

The **Bookmarks** button in Step 4 can also be used to access Reading List items. These are added from the **Share** button in Step 1, and enable items to be saved and read later, even if you are not connected to the internet. (The third button in Step 4 is for accessing your web browsing history.)

Using Tabs in Safari

In keeping with most modern web browsers, Safari uses tabs so that you can have several websites open at the same time. However, due to the fact that a smartphone's screen is smaller than the ones on a desktop or laptop computer, tabs operate in a specific way on the iPhone. To use tabs:

1 Open Safari and open a website. Tap once on this button on the bottom toolbar to view all currently-open tabs

2 Swipe up and down in Tab View to view all open tabs. Tap once on one to view that web page at full size

Press and hold on a tab to drag it into a different position in Tab View.

Press and hold the Tab button to get an option to close all open tabs in one action.

Don't forget

Tap once on the **Done** button at the bottom of the Tab View window to exit this and return to the web page that was being viewed when Tab View was activated.

3 Tap once on the **Tabs** button on the bottom toolbar to access options for viewing **Private** tabs (where no browsing details are stored) and also creating new tab groups

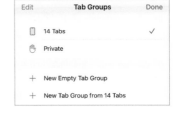

14 Tabs ∨

Opening tabs

To open more tabs in Safari on your iPhone:

1 Open the **Tab View** window as shown opposite, and tap once on this button

2 Open a new tab by entering a web address in the Address Bar, or by tapping once on one of the items in the **Favorites** window

Items that appear in the **Favorites** window can be specified with the Safari settings (**Settings** > **Safari** > **Favorites**) and by then selecting a category. This page will appear when a new tab is opened, and also when you tap in the Address Bar to enter a web address.

125

3 Swipe down the page to access items that are open on another one of your Apple devices – e.g. an iPad. Tap once on an item to open it in Safari

4 Tap once on this button to close any tab in Tab View

Setting Up an Email Account

Email accounts

Email settings can be specified within the Settings app. Different email accounts can also be added there.

It is possible to unsend an email if it has been sent in error, although this may not work if the recipient is not using iOS 16. To unsend an email, tap once on the **Undo Send** button at the bottom of the Mail window once an email has been sent. This can be done for up to 10 seconds after the email has been sent. This is a new feature in iOS 16.

Undo Send

1 Tap once on the **Settings** app

2 Tap once on the **Mail** tab

Mail

3 Tap once on the **Accounts** button

Accounts

4 Tap once on the **Add Account** button to add a new account

< Mail   **Accounts**

ACCOUNTS

iCloud
iCloud Drive, Mail, Contacts, Calendars and 8 more...

Add Account

5 Tap once on the type of email account you want to add

< Accounts   **Add Account**

iCloud
Microsoft Exchange
Google
yahoo!
Aol.
Outlook.com

Other

If your email provider is not on the **Add Account** list, tap once on **Other** at the bottom of the list and complete the account details using the information from your email provider.

6 Enter the details for the account, and tap on the **Next** button to move through the setup process

Cancel   accounts.google.com   AA

Google

Sign in

Use your Google Account

Let this iPhone access your mail and other Google Account data

Email or phone

Forgot email?

Create account   Next

7 Drag these buttons **On** or **Off** to specify which functions are to be available for the required account. Tap once on the **Save** button

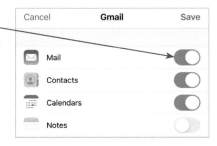

If you set up more than one email account, messages from all of them can be downloaded and displayed by **Mail**.

8 Each new account is added under the **Accounts** heading of the **Mail** section

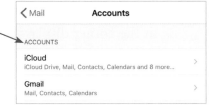

Email settings

Email settings can be specified within the Settings app.

1 Under the **Mail** section there are several options for how Mail operates and looks. These include how much of an email will be previewed in your Inbox, and options for accessing actions by swiping on an email

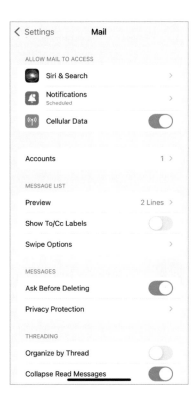

The **Organize by Thread** option can be turned **On** to show connected email conversations within your Inbox. If there is a thread of emails, this is indicated by this symbol:

Monday >

Tap on it once to view the thread.

Use these buttons at the top of the window when you are reading an email to view the next and previous messages:

To delete an email from your Inbox, swipe on it from right to left, and tap once on the **Trash/Delete** button.

If the **Fetch New Data** option in **Settings** > **Mail** > **Accounts** is set to **Push**, new emails will be downloaded automatically from your mail server. To check manually, swipe down from the top of the mailbox pane. The **Push** option uses up more battery power.

128

Emailing

Email on the iPhone is created, sent and received using the Mail app (although other email apps can be downloaded from the App Store). This provides a range of functionality for managing emails and responding to them.

Accessing Mail

To access Mail and start sending and receiving emails:

1 Tap once on the **Mail** app (the red icon in the corner displays the number of unread emails in your Inbox)

2 Tap once on a message to display it in the main panel

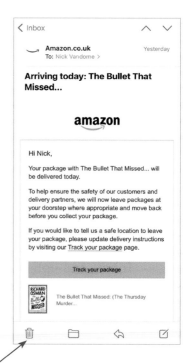

3 Use these buttons to, from left to right: delete a message; move a message to a different folder; or respond to a message (see the next page)

4 Tap once on this button to reply to a message, reply to everyone in a conversation, forward it to a new recipient, delete it, flag it, mark it as unread, or move it to a folder

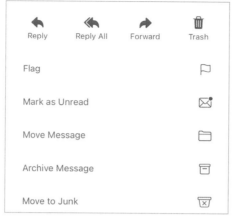

Reply   Reply All   Forward   Trash

Flag

Mark as Unread

Move Message

Archive Message

Move to Junk

Creating an email

To create and send an email:

1 Tap once on this button to create a new message

2 Enter a recipient name in the **To:** box

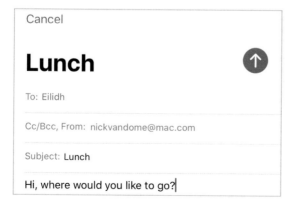

Cancel

Lunch

To: Eilidh

Cc/Bcc, From: nickvandome@mac.com

Subject: Lunch

Hi, where would you like to go?

3 Enter a subject and body text

4 Tap once on the **Send** button to send the email to the recipient

Hot tip

If the recipient is included in your Contacts app, their details will appear as you type in Step 2. Tap once on a name to add it in the **To:** box.

Hot tip

When writing an email, these buttons above the keyboard can be used to, from left to right: change the text size; add a photo; take a photo; scan a document; scan and insert text; add a document; or add a freehand sketch:

Aa

Video Chatting with FaceTime

Video chatting is a very personal and interactive way to keep in touch with family and friends around the world. To use FaceTime for video chatting:

1 Tap once on the **FaceTime** app

2 Tap once on the **New FaceTime** button

Don't forget

To make video calls with FaceTime you need an active internet connection and to be signed in with your Apple ID.

3 Enter the name of a contact in the **To:** box, or tap once on this button to select one from your Contacts app (or selected one of the **Suggested** options)

4 Use the Contacts app to select a contact

5 Tap once on the **FaceTime** video button to make a FaceTime call to another FaceTime user (the **Create Link** in Step 2 can be used to make FaceTime calls to non-FaceTime users – see page 133)

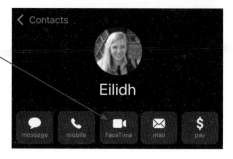

6 If a contact is added directly to the **To:** box in Step 3 on the opposite page, tap once on the **FaceTime** button to start a video call with them

Hot tip

Tap once on the **effects** button in Step 7 and tap once on this button to access any Memojis that you have created (see page 105). Tap once on one to superimpose it over your own face in the FaceTime window.

7 When you have connected, your contact appears in the main window and you appear in a picture-in-picture thumbnail in the corner

8 Use these buttons during a call to, from left to right: turn the speakers **On** or **Off**

; mute or unmute the microphone; turn the camera **On** or **Off** for the call (audio will still be available if the camera is **Off**); use SharePlay (see pages 134-135); and leave or end the call with the red button

9 Tap once on the **FaceTime** button in Step 8 to access more options for the call, including, from top to bottom: leaving the call; adding more people to the call; sharing links to the call for non-FaceTime users; show live captions (subtitles); and silencing requests from other people to join a FaceTime call

Hot tip

The **Share Link** option in Step 9 can be used to create FaceTime calls with non-FaceTime users, including those using the Windows and Android operating systems. See page 133 for details.

Don't forget

When you receive a FaceTime call, it appears as a small banner at the top of the screen. If the iPhone is locked, the call can be answered by swiping the **slide to answer** button from left to right on the Lock screen.

Don't forget

Spatial sound is used in group calls to present the sound as coming from the direction of the screen in which someone's FaceTime window is positioned, to create a more natural effect.

...cont'd

Receiving a FaceTime call

To answer a FaceTime call made to you by someone else:

1 Tap once the green video button to accept the call, or tap once on the red button to decline the call

2 After either of the options in Step 1 has been selected, tap once on the **Accept** button, or tap once on the **Remind Me** button, to get a reminder about the call instead of answering it

3 Tap once on the **Message** button in Step 2 to send a text message instead of answering a call

Microphone modes

FaceTime also has options for how the microphone operates.

1 Start a FaceTime call, access the Control Center (see page 46) and tap once on the **Mic Mode** button

2 Tap once on the **Voice Isolation** button to block out background noise and give clearer prominence to the current speaker in a call

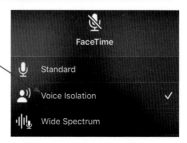

Creating a FaceTime link

Before iOS 15, it was only possible to use FaceTime to make video calls to other FaceTime users using an Apple device. However, iOS 15 made it possible for you to send a link to anyone, who can then join the FaceTime call via the web, and this continues with iOS 16. To do this:

1 Open the FaceTime app and tap once on the **Create Link** button

It is also possible to invite someone to an existing FaceTime call, via a link, using the **Share Link** button in Step 9 on page 131.

2 Select an option for how you want to send the link to join the FaceTime call – e.g. by email

When someone receives an invitation to join a FaceTime call, the recipient can tap once on the **FaceTime Link** button in the invitation, enter their name and tap once on the **Continue** button.

3 Compose an invitation in the app selected in Step 2 and send it to the recipient

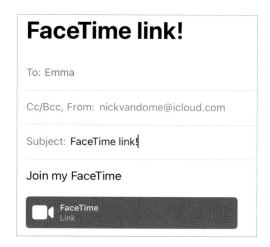

...cont'd

Using SharePlay in FaceTime

SharePlay is a function within FaceTime that enables you to share your screen and play movies, TV shows and music, and share this content with other people on a FaceTime call. To do this:

Content for SharePlay is synchronized for everyone in a FaceTime call, so everyone sees and hears the same content at the same time.

1 Access **Settings > FaceTime > SharePlay** and drag the **SharePlay** button **On**

2 Start a FaceTime call and tap once on this button on the FaceTime control panel to share your iPhone screen with everyone else on an existing call

3 Tap once on the **Share My Screen** button

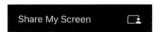

4 When a screen is being shared in a FaceTime call with SharePlay, whatever is shown on the sharing screen will be visible on everyone else's screen too. This appears as a separate panel, and the user's video feed is automatically turned off

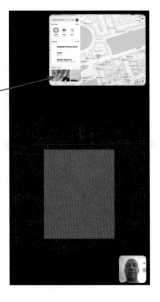

Sharing music, movies or TV shows

SharePlay can also be used to share content with other people on a FaceTime call from the Music app and the TV app. To do this:

1 Start a FaceTime call and open either the **Music** app or the **TV** app. For either one, open the item you want to share on the FaceTime call

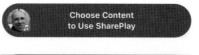

2 For music, tap once on the **SharePlay** button and select how you want to start sharing music each time

3 For the **TV** app, select how you want to use an item you are opening – e.g. use it with SharePlay so that people on the FaceTime call can see it, or just open it for yourself on your iPhone

4 Content from the **TV** app that is used with SharePlay plays within the FaceTime interface, and everyone on the call will be able to view it at the same time

Hot tip

If content is being shared with SharePlay from the TV app, all participants can use the TV app controls – e.g. everyone can pause/play, rewind or fast forward, and this will apply for everyone in the call.

Hot tip

The controls at the top of the window in Step 4 can be used to make the content full-screen, and adjust the volume. This only affects the device on which changes are being made, not for everyone in the call.

Adding Social Media

Using social media sites such as Facebook, Twitter, Instagram, and Snapchat to keep in touch with family and friends has now become common across all generations. On the iPhone with iOS 16, it is possible to link to these accounts so that you can share content to them from your iPhone, and also view updates through the Notification Center. To add social media apps to your iPhone:

Don't forget

Social media sites can be accessed from their own apps on the iPhone, and also from their respective websites, using Safari.

1 Open the App Store and navigate to the **Apps > Categories > Social Networking** section

Hot tip

Check out Facebook for Seniors in easy steps for more help with using this app, at www.ineasysteps.com

2 Tap once on the required apps to download them to your iPhone

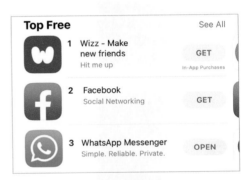

Top Free   See All

1 Wizz – Make new friends
  Hit me up   **GET**
                                   In-App Purchases

2 Facebook
  Social Networking   **GET**

3 WhatsApp Messenger
  Simple. Reliable. Private.   **OPEN**

3 Tap once on an app to open it

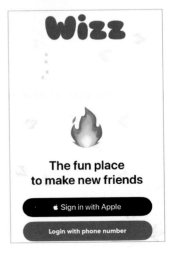

Hot tip

Updates can be set to appear in your **Notification Center**. Open **Settings**, and tap once on the **Notifications** tab. Under the **Notification Style** heading, tap once on the social media site and select options for how you would like the notifications to appear.

4 If you already have an account with the social media service, enter your login details or create a new account, as required

Wizz

The fun place to make new friends

 Sign in with Apple

Login with phone number

8 Hands on with Apps

Apps provide the iPhone with its functionality. This chapter details the built-in apps, and also shows how to access those in the App Store.

You need an active internet connection to download apps from the App Store.

Within a number of apps there is a **Share** button that can be used to share items through a variety of methods, including Messages, email, Facebook and Twitter.

What is an App?

An app is just a more modern name for a computer program. Initially, it was used in relation to mobile devices such as the iPhone and the iPad, but it is now becoming more widely used with desktop and laptop computers, for both Mac and Windows operating systems.

On the iPhone there are two types of apps:

- **Built-in apps**. These are the apps that come already installed on the iPhone.

- **App Store apps**. These are apps that can be downloaded from the online App Store. There is a huge range of apps available there, covering a variety of different categories. Some are free, while others have to be paid for. The apps in the App Store are updated and added to on a daily basis, so there are always new ones to explore.

There are also two important points about apps (both built-in and those from the App Store) to remember:

- Apart from some of the built-in apps, the majority of apps do not interact with each other. This means that there is less chance of viruses being transmitted from app to app on your iPhone, and they can operate without a reliance on other apps.

- Content created by apps is saved within the app itself, rather than within a file structure on your iPhone – e.g. if you create a note in the Notes app, it is saved there; if you take a photo, it is saved in the Photos app. Content is usually also saved automatically when it is created or edited, so you do not have to worry about saving it as you work on it.

Built-in Apps

The built-in iPhone apps are the ones that appear on the Home screen when you first get your iPhone.

Hot tip

- **App Store**. This can be used to access the online App Store, from where additional apps can be downloaded and updated.

- **Books**. This is an app for downloading electronic books, which can then be read on the iPhone.

- **Calculator**. This is a basic calculator, which can also be accessed from the Control Center.

- **Calendar**. An app for storing appointments, important dates, and other calendar information. It can be synced with iCloud.

- **Camera**. This gives direct access to the front-facing and rear-facing iPhone cameras.

- **Clock**. This displays the current time, and can be used to view the time in different countries. It also has an alarm clock and a stopwatch.

- **Compass**. This can be used to show you the direction of North. You can give the compass access to your location so that you can follow it from where you are.

- **Contacts**. An address book app. Once contacts are added here they can then also be accessed from other apps, such as Mail.

- **FaceTime**. This app uses the front-facing FaceTime camera to hold video or audio chats with people using a variety of devices.

- **Files**. This is used to back up items and make them available to other Apple devices.

When you first open some apps they will display options for location access; i.e. whether the app can access your current location. The options are for: allowing access while using the app; allowing access once; or not allowing access. If you select to allow access once, you will be prompted with the same query the next time you use the app. This is designed to prevent apps from constantly having access to your location. Location settings can also be applied in **Settings > Privacy & Security > Location Services**.

Hot tip

If you don't want your contacts to be accessed by other apps, open **Settings > Privacy & Security > Contacts** and drag the buttons **Off**.

...cont'd

Although iTunes has been removed from Mac computers with the macOS operating system, the iTunes Store is still a part of iOS 16 and can be used to download a range of content, including music and movies. These items are then displayed in their respective apps – e.g. the Music and TV apps, which can both access content too.

Check out Smart Homes in easy steps for more help with the Home app, at www. ineasysteps.com

You need an Apple ID to obtain content from the iTunes Store and the Book Store.

140

- **Find My**. This can be used to view the location of family and friends, based on their Apple mobile devices and Mac computers. See pages 184-185.

- **Health**. This stores and collates a range of health information. See pages 157-159.

- **Home**. This can be used to control certain compatible functions within the home, such as heating controls.

- **iTunes Store**. This app can be used to browse the iTunes Store, where content can be downloaded to your iPhone.

- **Mail**. This is the email app for sending and receiving email on your iPhone.

- **Maps**. Use this app to view maps from around the world, find specific locations, and get directions to destinations.

- **Measure**. This can be used to measure the length or perimeter of items.

- **Messages**. This is the iPhone messaging service, which can be used for SMS text messages and iMessages between compatible Apple devices.

- **Music**. An app for playing music on your iPhone and also viewing cover artwork. You can also use it to create your own playlists.

- **News**. This collates news stories from numerous online publications and categories.

- **Notes**. If you need to jot down your thoughts or ideas, this app is just perfect for that.

- **Photos**. This is an app for viewing, editing and sharing your photos and videos.

- **Podcasts**. This can be used to download podcasts from within the App Store.

- **Reminders**. Use this app to help keep organized, when you want to create to-do lists and set reminders for events.

- **Safari**. The Apple web browser that has been developed for viewing the web on your iPhone.

- **Settings**. This contains a range of settings for the iPhone (see pages 20-21 for details).

- **Stocks**. Use this to display the latest stock market prices and add your own companies.

- **Tips**. This can be used to display tips and hints for items on your iPhone.

- **Translate**. This can be used for translations in real-time conversations, using 11 languages.

- **TV**. This is an app for viewing videos from the TV Store, and also streaming them to a larger HDTV monitor.

- **Voice Memos**. This can be used to record short audio reminders that can be stored and played on the iPhone.

- **Wallet**. This can be used to store credit, debit, and store card details, for making payments with Apple Pay (in some locations). It can also be used for storing coupons, boarding passes, event tickets and more.

- **Watch**. This can be used to pair an iPhone with the Apple Watch and apply a range of settings.

- **Weather**. Displays weather details for your location and destinations around the world.

Podcasts are audio or video programs, and they cover an extensive range of subjects.

The TV app can also be used to access the Apple TV+ service. This is a subscription service for streaming original TV shows and movies from Apple TV.

About the App Store

While the built-in apps that come with the iPhone are flexible and versatile, apps really come into their own when you connect to the App Store. This is an online resource, and there are thousands of apps there that can be downloaded and then used on your iPhone, including categories from Lifestyle to Medical and Travel.

To use the App Store, you must first have an Apple ID. This can be obtained when you first connect to the App Store if you don't already have one. Once you have an Apple ID, you can start exploring the App Store and the apps within it.

1 Tap once on the **App Store** app on the Home screen

2 The latest available apps are displayed on the Homepage of the App Store, including the featured and best new apps

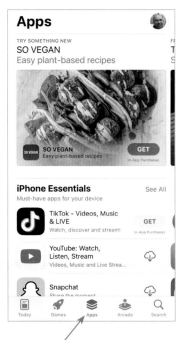

The items within the **Today** section of the App Store change on a regular basis, so it is always worth looking at it from time to time.

3 Tap on these buttons to view items according to **Today**, **Games**, **Apps**, **Arcade** and **Search**

Viewing apps

To view apps in the App Store and read about their content and functionality:

1 Tap once on an app

2 General details about the app are displayed

3 Swipe left or right here to view additional information about the app

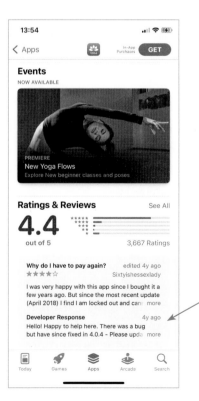

If it is an upgraded version of an app, this page will include details of any fixes and improvements that have been made.

4 Scroll down the page to see additional information including reviews and new items in this version of the app

Some apps will differ depending on the geographical location from which you are accessing the App Store.

There are an increasing number of Augmented Reality (AR) apps in the App Store. These are apps that combine real-life images, either within the app or from the device's camera, that are used with graphical elements; e.g. constellations can be drawn over an image of the sky in an astronomy app.

Finding Apps

Featured

Within the App Store, apps are separated into categories according to type. This enables you to find apps according to particular subjects. To do this:

1 Tap once on the **Apps** button on the toolbar at the bottom of the App Store

2 Scroll up and down to view all of the sections within the Apps Homepage, and scroll left and right to view items within each section heading

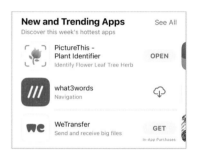

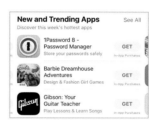

3 Scroll down the page to the **Top Categories** section, and tap once on the **See All** button to view the full range of categories of apps

4 Tap once on a category to view the items within it. This can be navigated in the same way as the main Homepage in the App Store; e.g. swipe up and down to view sections, and left and right on each panel to view the available apps

Top Charts

To find the top-rated apps:

1 Tap once on the **Apps** button on the toolbar at the bottom of the App Store

2 Scroll down the page to view **Top Free** and **Top Paid** apps

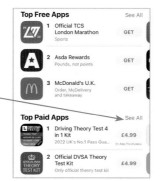

3 Tap once on the **See All** button to view all **Top Paid** or **Top Charts** apps

Do not limit yourself to just viewing the top apps. Although these are the most popular, there are also a lot of excellent apps within each category.

Searching for apps

Another way to find apps is with the App Store Search box, which appears at the top of the App Store window once it has been accessed. To use this to find apps:

1 Tap once on the **Search** button at the bottom of the window to access the Search box

2 Tap in the Search box to activate the keyboard and enter a search keyword or phrase

For more information about using the iPhone virtual keyboard, see pages 92-101.

3 Suggested apps appear as you are typing

4 Tap on an app to view it

Downloading Apps

When you identify an app that you would like to use, it can be downloaded to your iPhone. To do this:

Don't forget

Apps usually download in a few minutes or less, depending on the speed of your Wi-Fi connection.

Beware

Some apps have "in-app purchases". This is additional content that has to be paid for when it is downloaded.

1 Find the app you want, using the **App Store**

2 Tap once on the **Price** or **Get** button

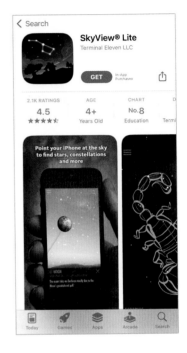

3 If Face ID is used on the phone, double-click the side button. (For iPhones with a Home button, press on the Home button with the finger that was used to set up Touch ID)

4 The app is downloaded to the next available space on the Home screen or is put in the relevant folder in the App Library (see pages 34-35)

Updating Apps

The publishers of apps provide updates that bring new features and improvements. You do not have to check your apps to see if there are updates – you can set them to be updated automatically through the Settings app. To do this:

1 Open **Settings** and tap on the **App Store** tab

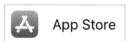

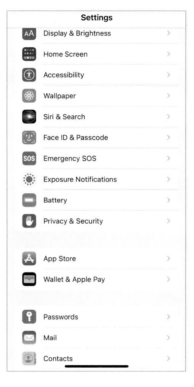

Hot tip

You should keep your apps as up-to-date as possible to take advantage of software fixes and any updates to the iPhone operating system (iOS).

2 Under **Automatic Downloads**, drag the **App Updates** button **On** to enable automatic updates for apps

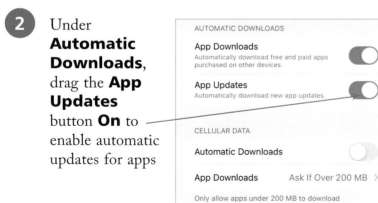

Managing your Apps

As more apps are added it can become hard to find the ones you want, particularly if you have to swipe between several screens. However, it is possible to organize apps into individual folders to make using them more manageable. To do this:

1 Press on an app until it starts to jiggle and the **−** symbol appears in the top left-hand corner

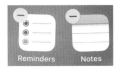

2 Drag the app over another one

3 A folder is created, containing the two apps. The folder is given a default name, usually based on the category of the first app

148

4 Tap once on the folder name and type a new name, if required

5 Tap on the **done** button on the keyboard to finish creating the folder

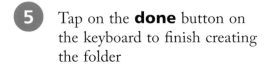

6 The folder is added on the Home screen. Tap on this to access the items within it (press and hold on it to move it)

9 Apps for Every Day

The iPhone has apps for all aspects of your daily life, including listening to music, staying healthy, keeping notes, organizing calendars, and reading the news.

Around the iTunes Store

The iPhone performs an excellent role as a mobile entertainment center: its versatility means that you can carry your music, videos, and books in your pocket. Much of this content comes from the online iTunes Store. To access this and start adding content to your iPhone:

Although iTunes has been removed from Mac computers with the macOS operating system, the iTunes Store is still a part of iOS 16 and can be used to download a range of content, including music and movies. These items are then displayed in their respective apps; e.g. the Music and TV apps.

1 Tap once on the **iTunes Store** app

iTunes Store

2 The iTunes Store interface is similar to the App Store. Tap once on the **Featured** or **Charts** tab at the top of the window to view these headings

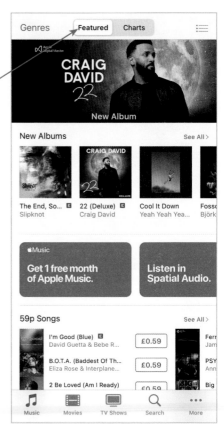

Tap once on the **Genres** button at the top of the Music Homepage to view items for different musical genres and styles.

Genres

Downloaded movies and TV shows take up a lot of storage space on the iPhone.

3 Use the buttons on the bottom toolbar to access content for **Music**, **Movies** and **TV Shows**

4 Swipe to the left and right on each panel to view items within it

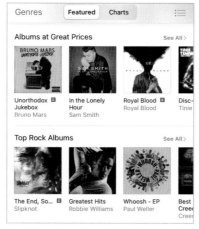

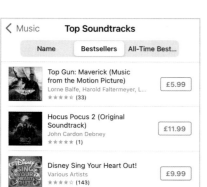

Tap once on the **Charts** tab at the top of the **iTunes Store** window to view the top-ranking items for the category that is being viewed.

Charts

5 Swipe up and down to view more headings

6 Tap once on the **Movies** button to view the movies in the iTunes Store. These can be bought or rented

7 Tap once on the **TV Shows** button to view the TV shows in the iTunes Store. These can be bought or rented

To view all of your iTunes purchases, tap once on the **More** button on the bottom toolbar and tap once on the **Purchased** button. View your purchases by category (Music, Films/Movies or TV Programmes/Shows), and tap once on the cloud symbol next to a purchased item to download it to your iPhone.

8 Tap once on the **More** button to access additional content

9 Tap once on the **Genius** button to view suggested content, based on what you have already bought from the iTunes Store

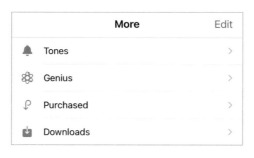

Buying Items

Once you have found the content you want in the iTunes Store, you can then buy it and download it to your iPhone.

Don't forget

If you have set up Apple Pay (see pages 62-63) you will be able to use this to buy items in the iTunes Store. You can also record debit/credit card details in your Apple ID account to pay for items. Use the Face ID function (see page 24) to authorize the payment using Apple Pay.

1 For music items, tap once on the price button next to an item (either an album or individual songs) and follow the instructions. Tap once on the **Music** app to play the item (see pages 153-155)

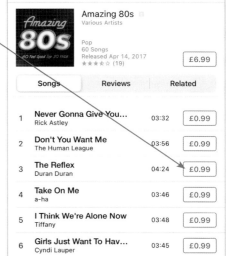

< Music

Amazing 80s
Various Artists

Pop
60 Songs
Released Apr 14, 2017
★★★☆☆ (19)

£6.99

Songs · Reviews · Related

1	Never Gonna Give You... Rick Astley	03:32	£0.99
2	Don't You Want Me The Human League	03:56	£0.99
3	The Reflex Duran Duran	04:24	£0.99
4	Take On Me a-ha	03:46	£0.99
5	I Think We're Alone Now Tiffany	03:48	£0.99
6	Girls Just Want To Hav... Cyndi Lauper	03:45	£0.99

Don't forget

For rented movies and TV shows, you have 30 days to watch an item after you have downloaded it. After you have started watching, you have 48 hours until it expires.

2 For movies and TV shows, tap once on the **Buy** or **Rent** button next to the title. Tap once on the **TV** app to play the item

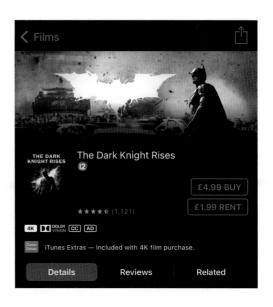

< Films

THE DARK KNIGHT RISES

The Dark Knight Rises
12

★★★★☆ (1,121)

£4.99 BUY
£1.99 RENT

4K DOLBY VISION CC AD

iTunes Extras — Included with 4K film purchase.

Details · Reviews · Related

Music on the iPhone

Once music has been bought from the iTunes Store, it can be played on your iPhone using the Music app. To do this:

1 Tap once on the **Music** app

2 Tap once on the **Library** button on the bottom toolbar

Hot tip

To create a playlist of songs, tap once on the **Playlists** button in Step 3, then tap once on the **New Playlist...** button. Give it a name and then add songs from your Library, using the **Add Music** button.

3 Select one of the options for viewing items in the Library. These include **Playlists**, **Artists**, **Albums**, **Songs**, and **Downloaded**. The list of options showing on the **Library** page can be edited using the **Edit** button

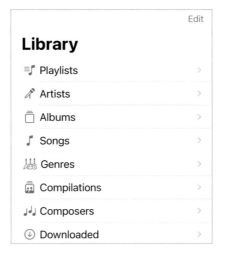

4 For the **Artists** section, tap once on an artist to view details of their songs on your iPhone

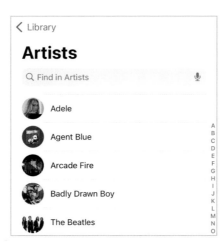

153

...cont'd

Tap once on this button in the top right-hand corner in Step 7 to access a menu for the current track: This includes options to download the track, delete it from the Music app Library, add it to a playlist, or share it.

By default, music that has been bought from the iTunes Store is kept online and can be played on your iPhone by streaming it over Wi-Fi. However, it is also possible to download tracks to your iPhone so that you can play them without being online. Tap once on this button to download a specific track:

⑤ Select a track to play it

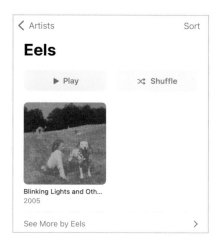

⑥ A limited version of the music controls appears at the bottom of the window

⑦ Tap once here to view the full version of the music controls. Use these buttons to return to the start of a track, play/pause a track, fast-forward, and adjust the volume

Using Apple Music

Apple Music is a service that makes the entire Apple iTunes Library of music available to users. It is a subscription service, but there is a three-month free trial. Music can be streamed over the internet or downloaded so that you can listen to it when you are offline. To start with Apple Music:

1 Tap once on the **Music** app

2 Tap once on the **Listen Now** button

3 Tap once on the **Try It Free** button to activate a three-month free trial of Apple Music

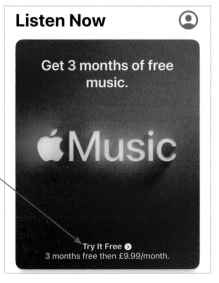

Hot tip

To end your Apple Music subscription at any point (and to ensure you do not subscribe at the end of the free trial), open the **Settings** app. Tap once on the **Apple ID, iCloud, Media & Purchases** button, and tap once on the **Subscriptions** button. Under **Subscriptions**, tap once on the Apple Music subscription and tap once on the **Cancel Subscription** button. By default, subscriptions renew automatically if they are not canceled.

4 After the three-month free trial there will be an option to **Choose Your Plan** if you want to continue with Apple Music, and pay a subscription. The options are **Individual**, **Student** or **Family**. Select one of the options and tap once on the **Join Apple Music** button. Once you have joined Apple Music, you will be able to listen to the entire Apple Music Library

Apple Watch with the iPhone

The Apple Watch has now reached its seventh version: Apple Watch Series 8. This is much more than a watch, though; it is also a body monitoring device. It has a number of sensors on the back, which monitor information such as heart rate and body movement. There is also an activity app to measure your fitness activities. A lot of this data can be sent to the Health app on the iPhone, where it can be stored and analyzed in greater depth.

The Apple Watch Series 8 has an always-on display (some of the previous versions only showed the display when the watch on the wearer's wrist was moved toward their face), a battery life of up to 18 hours before a charge is required, and a fast charging capability.

Some previous versions of the Apple Watch had to be paired (linked) with the iPhone to access certain functionality, such as making and receiving calls. Although the Apple Watch can make calls through its own cellular connectivity, it is best to pair it with the Watch app.

The Apple Watch Series 8 also has a host of useful apps and features, aimed at improving health and fitness: there is an Electrocardiogram (ECG) app that includes an electrical heart sensor that can show your heart rhythm; blood oxygen sensors for measuring your blood oxygen levels; built-in fall detection that can alert an emergency contact if you have a fall; crash detection for alerting the emergency services if you are in a car accident; a Sleep app for monitoring your sleep patterns; and an enhanced Workout app for monitoring daily exercise routines. The Apple Watch Series 8 also includes a Maps app, which is ideal for displaying directions when you are out and about.

There is also a wide range of interchangeable bands that can be used with the Apple Watch so that you can customize it just the way you want.

Don't forget

The Apple Watch is "paired" with an iPhone using the Watch app.

Watch

Hot tip

The App Store has a **Health & Fitness** category and also a **Medical** category, to cover a wide range of health-related issues. Many of the apps can be used with the Apple Watch. There is also an **Apple Watch Apps** category.

Beware

If you have a pre-existing medical condition or are on any medication, always consult your doctor before using a new health or fitness app that could have an impact on this.

Using the Health App

The Health app is available in iOS 16, and it enables you to input and analyze a wide range of health and fitness information. There are two main areas within the app.

Health

Hot tip

Summary

This displays an overview of items that have been specified to appear here. To use this:

1

Tap once on the **Summary** button on the bottom toolbar

Summary

2

Summary information is displayed for a range of health and fitness categories

Items that appear on the **Summary** page can be edited, by tapping once on the **Edit** button in Step 1. On the **Edit Favorites** page, tap once next to the items that you want to appear, so that they have a solid star next to them.

3

Tap once on an item to view more details about it

...cont'd

Browse

This displays the available categories within the Health app, and shows any data that has been added for them.

Beware

When adding data, do so at regular intervals, to build up a comprehensive set of results for analysis by the Health app.

1 Tap once on the **Browse** button on the bottom toolbar

2 A range of health and fitness categories is displayed. Swipe down the page to view more items

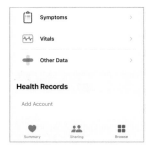

Hot tip

In addition to fitness categories, a range of medical information can also be entered and stored in the Health app, including specific medical conditions and immunizations.

3 Tap once on an item to view fuller details

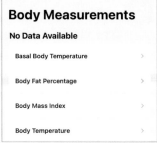

4 For each item, health data can be entered manually (see the next page)

Adding health data

To enter data for the categories in the Health app:

1 Tap once on the **Summary** button

2 Tap once on one of the categories on the Summary page

3 Tap once on the **Add Data** button

Add Data

4 Enter details for the selected item; e.g. entering the type and duration of a specific workout. Tap once on the **Add** button

5 The data is added for the selected item, and this will be collated and stored within the Health app. Tap on these buttons to view the data for **Day**, **Week**, **Month**, **6 months**, and **Year**. Tap once on the **Summary** button to return to the main Summary page

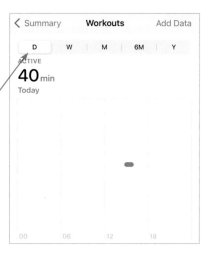

< Summary

Hot tip

Health data can be added for the full range of categories in the **Browse** section by tapping once on the **Add Data** button in Step 4 on the previous page.

Don't forget

Some items in the Health app have data added automatically, such as Walking + Running Distance, Steps, and Flights Climbed, in the Activity category.

Jotting Down Notes

It is always useful to have a quick way of making notes of everyday things, such as shopping lists, recipes, or packing lists for traveling. On your iPhone, the Notes app is perfect for this function. To use it:

160

1 Tap once on the **Notes** app

2 Tap once on this button on the bottom toolbar to create a new note

3 Enter text for the note. The first line of a note becomes its title in the left-hand **Notes** panel

4 The toolbar above the keyboard can be used for adding content to the note. (Tap once on the cross to close the toolbar)

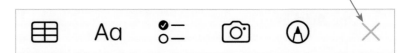

5 Double-tap on text to select it, and tap once on this button to access text formatting options

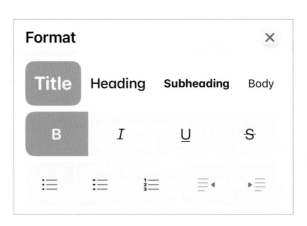

6 Tap once on this button to create a checklist. Add items to the list. Tap once on a check button to add a check mark and show it as completed

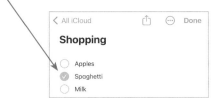

7 Tap once on this button to add a handwritten item or drawing

8 Tap once on this button to add a photo or video to a note. Select a photo or video from your Library, or take a new one

Choose Photo or Video	🖼
Scan Documents	🗔
Take Photo or Video	📷
Scan Text	🗐

9 By default, the most recently-created or edited note appears at the top of the Notes panel. However, it is possible to pin your most frequently-used notes to the top of this panel. To do this: in the main Notes screen, press and hold on the note to be pinned and tap once on the **Pin Note** button.
The note is pinned at the top of the **Notes** panel

Pin Note	📌
Lock Note	🔒
Share Note	👥
Send a Copy	⬆
Move	🗀
Delete	🗑

Don't forget

For more information about selecting text, see page 101.

Don't forget

Tap once on this button on the top toolbar of a note to access a range of options for the note:
These include options for: scanning items into a note; pinning a note; locking a note; or deleting it. There are also options for: sharing the current note; searching for items; moving a note to a folder within the Notes app; and applying lines and grids over a note.

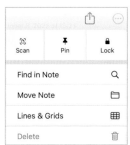

161

Keeping Up-to-Date

The Calendar app can be used to add events and appointments and keep yourself up-to-date with your daily, weekly, monthly, and annual activities.

1 Tap once on the **Calendar** app

2 If **Month** view is displayed, tap once here to access **Year** view. In Year view, tap once on a month to view it

3 Tap once on a day to view it (the current day is highlighted in red)

Hot tip

Tap once on the **Today** button from any date to view the current date, in whichever view you are currently in.

Today

4 Tap once on this button to view the calendar and any events that have been added, within the same window

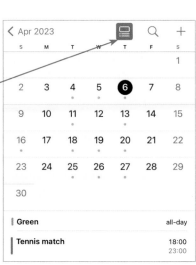

Adding events

To add new events to the calendar:

1 Press and hold on a time slot within Day view, or tap once on this button

2 Enter a title for the event, and tap once on the **Starts** button to add a start time. Tap once on the time and enter a new time, as required

3 Add an end time by tapping on the **Ends** button, and also a repeat frequency (for recurring events such as birthdays). Select a specific calendar for the event and add an alert, if required. Tap once on the **Add** button to create the event

4 Tap once on this button to view a list of your current events and appointments

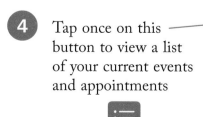

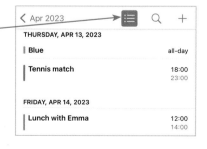

Hot tip

Drag the **All-day** button **On** to set an event for the whole day, rather than adding specific start and end times.

Don't forget

The repeat frequency for an event can be set to every day, every week, every 2 weeks, every month, or every year. There is also a **Custom** option for specific time periods.

163

Getting the News

The iPhone with iOS 16 is ideal for keeping up with the news, whether you are on the move or at home. This is made even easier with the News app, which can be used to collate news stories from numerous online media outlets, covering hundreds of subjects. To use it:

Hot tip

Tap once on the **News+** button on the bottom toolbar to access Apple's subscription service for the News app.

News+

Hot tip

To delete an item from the **Following** section, tap once on the **Edit** button in the top right-hand corner, and tap once on the red circle next to the item you want to delete. This will remove its related content from your news feed.

1 Tap once on the **News** app

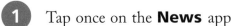

News

2 Tap once on the **Today** button on the bottom toolbar to view the latest stories in your news feed

Today

3 The latest news stories are displayed. Swipe up the page to view specific categories, such as **For You**

4 Tap once on the **Following** button on the bottom toolbar to view subjects or publications that you are following; i.e. they are used to populate your news feed

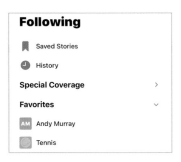

Following

10 On the Go

The iPhone is a great companion whenever you are out and about anywhere, whether at home or abroad.

Finding Locations

Finding locations around the world is only ever a couple of taps away when you have your iPhone and the Maps app.

1 Tap once on the **Maps** app

2 The Search box is at the bottom of the window

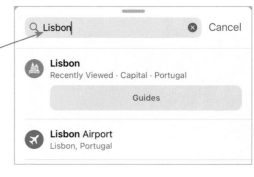

Hot tip

The Maps app works best if you have **Location Services** turned **On**, so that it can show your current location and give directions in relation to this. To turn on Location Services, go to **Settings** > **Privacy & Security** > **Location Services** > **Maps** and tap once on **While Using the App**.

166

3 Enter an item into the Search box. As you type, suggestions appear underneath. Tap on one to go to that location

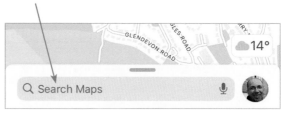

4 For the current location, swipe up for options for searching over items such as food outlets, shops, and entertainment. Tap on one of these to see results for these categories in the current location

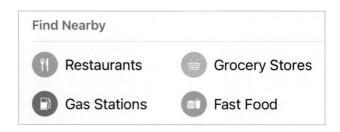

5 The location selected in Step 3 on the previous page is displayed, with information about it at the bottom of the window

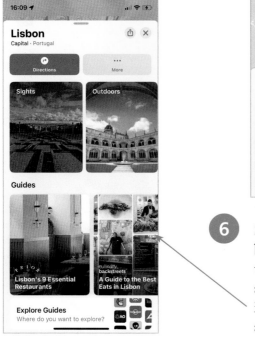

If a specific street is being viewed, tap once on this icon to view the location in street view, which provides a photographic interface from where you can explore the location:

6 Swipe up from the bottom of the window to view full details about the location, including photos, address, phone number, and website address, if available

Some locations have a **3D Flyover Tour** feature. This is an automated tour of a location, featuring its most notable sites. It covers major cities around the world, and the list is regularly being added to. If it is available for a location, tap once on the **Flyover** button at the bottom of the window, next to the **Directions** button. Tap once on the **Start Tour** button to start the Flyover Tour. Try it with a location such as New York, London or Paris.

7 At the top of the Maps app window, tap once on this icon for map style options

8 Select either **Explore**, **Driving**, **Transit** or **Satellite** to view the map in that style

Getting Directions

Wherever you are in the world, you can get directions between two locations. To do this:

Hot tip

You can enter the **Start** point as your current location. Tap once on this button to view your current location:

Beware

If you enter the name of a landmark you may also be shown other items that have the same name, such as businesses.

Hot tip

For some destinations, alternative routes will be displayed, depending on distance and traffic conditions. Tap once on an alternative route to select it. Directions for each route can be selected at the bottom of the window.

1 Tap once in the Search box at the bottom of the window in the Maps app

2 Enter the destination (by default, this is from your current location)

3 Tap once on this button. The route is shown on the map

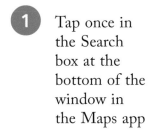

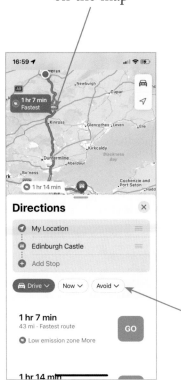

4 Tap once on these buttons to select options for the route, including a start time and any items to avoid during transit along the route

5 Tap once on the **Go** button to view step-by-step instructions on the map

6 The route is displayed, from your starting location. Audio instructions tell you the directions to be followed. You can use the **Volume** buttons (on the side of the iPhone) to increase or decrease the sound. As you follow the route, the map and instructions are updated

7 Swipe up from the bottom of the screen to access options for adding a stop on the way, sharing your estimated time of arrival (ETA) and reporting an issue

Don't forget

Tap once on the **End Route** button to stop following the current route.

8 Tap once on the **Add Stop** button in Step 7 to view suitable nearby locations

Booking a Trip

Most major travel retailers have had their own websites for a number of years. They have now moved into the world of apps, and these can be used on your iPhone to book almost any type of vacation, from cruises to city breaks.

Several apps for the iPhone (and their associated websites) offer full travel services where they can deal with flights, hotels, insurance, car hire, and excursions. These include:

- **Expedia**
- **KAYAK**
- **Orbitz**
- **Travelocity**

These apps usually list special offers and last-minute deals on their Homepages, and they offer options for booking flights, hotels, car hire, and activities separately.

Hot tip

It is always worth searching different apps to get the best possible price. In some cases, it is cheapest to buy different elements of a vacation from different retailers; e.g. flights from one seller and accommodation from another.

Don't forget

Most travel apps have specific versions based on your geographical location. You will be directed to these by default.

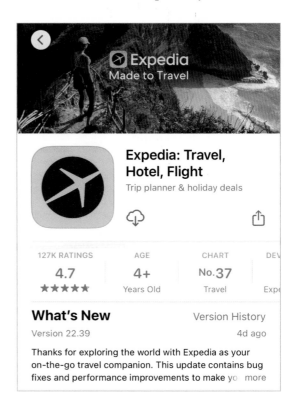

Tripadvisor

One of the best resources for travelers is **Tripadvisor**. Not only does the app provide a full range of opportunities for booking flights and hotels, but it also has an extensive network of reviews from people who have visited the countries, hotels, and restaurants on the site. These are independent, and usually very fair and honest. In a lot of cases, if there are issues with a hotel or restaurant, the proprietor posts a reply to explain what is being done to address any problems.

Tripadvisor has a certain sense of community, so post your own reviews once you have been places to let others know about your experience.

Cruises

There are also apps dedicated specifically to cruises. One to look at is **My Kind of Cruise**, which searches over a range of companies for your perfect cruise vacation.

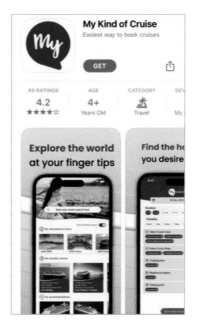

Booking Hotels

The internet is a perfect vehicle for finding good-value hotel rooms around the world. When hotels have spare capacity, this can quickly be relayed to associated websites and apps, where users can often benefit from cheap prices and special offers. There are plenty of apps that have details of thousands of hotels around the world, such as:

Trivago

An app that searches over 1 million hotels on more than 250 sites, to ensure you get the right hotel for the best price.

Hotels.com

A stylish app that enables you to enter search keywords into a Search box on the Home screen to find hotels based on destination, name, or local landmarks.

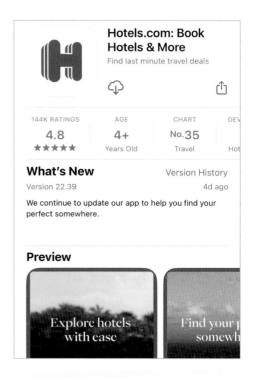

Booking.com

Another good, fully-featured hotel app that provides a comprehensive service and excellent prices.

HotelTonight

An app that specializes in getting the best deals for hotels around the world. Some genuine bargains can be found here, for hotels of all categories.

Hot tip

Most hotel apps have reviews of all of the listed establishments. It is always worth reading these, as it gives you a view from people who have actually been there.

Hot tip

Currency converters can also be downloaded from the App Store so that you can see how much your money is worth in different countries.

Finding Flights

Flying is a common part of modern life and although you do not have to book separate flights for a vacation (if it is part of a package), there are a number of apps for booking flights and also for following the progress of those in the air.

Skyscanner – travel deals

This app can be used to find flights at airports around the world. Enter your details such as leaving airport, destination and dates of travel. The results show a range of available options, covering different price ranges and airlines.

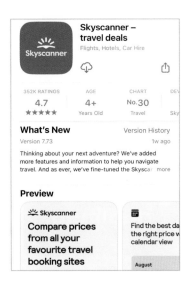

Flight apps need to have an internet connection in order to show real-time flight information.

Flightradar24

If you like viewing the path of flights that are in the air, or need to check if flights are going to be delayed, this app provides this inflight information. Flights are shown according to flight number and airline.

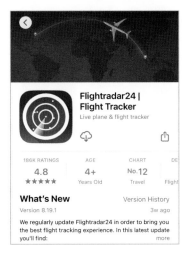

FlightAware Flight Tracker

Another app for tracking flights, showing arrivals and departures and also information about delays. It can track commercial flights worldwide.

Speaking their Language

When you are traveling abroad, it is always beneficial to learn some of the language of the country you are visiting. With your iPhone at hand, this has become a whole lot easier, and there are a number of options.

Don't forget

The iPhone also has its own built-in **Translate** app.

Beware

Some language apps are free, but they then charge for additional content, known as "in-app purchases".

1 Translation apps that can be used to translate words, phrases and sentences in every language you probably need

2 Language apps that offer options in several languages

3 Specific language apps, where you can fully get to grips with a new language

⑪ Practical Matters

This chapter looks at accessibility, screen time issues and security.

Accessibility Issues

The iPhone tries to cater to as wide a range of users as possible, including those who have difficulty with vision or hearing and those who have physical and motor issues. There are a number of settings that can help with these areas. To access the range of **Accessibility** settings:

Don't forget

You will have to scroll down the page to view the full range of **Accessibility** options.

1 Tap once on the **Settings** app

2 Tap once on the **Accessibility** tab

3 The settings for **Vision**, **Physical and Motor**, **Hearing**, and **General** are displayed here

Hot tip

Tap once on **Accessibility** > **Display & Text Size** and drag the **On/Off Labels** button **On** to show the relevant icons on the **On/Off** buttons.

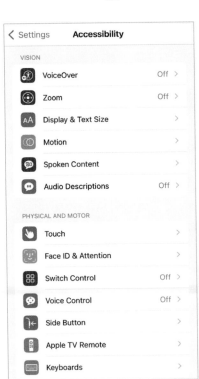

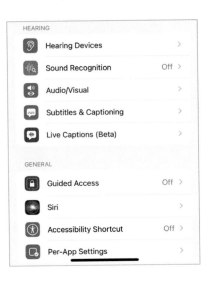

Vision settings

These can help anyone with impaired vision. There are options to hear items on the screen and also for making text easier to read.

1 Tap once on the **VoiceOver** link

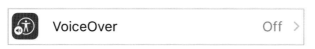

2 Drag this button **On** to activate the **VoiceOver** function. This then enables items to be spoken when you tap on them

3 Select options for **VoiceOver** as required, such as speaking rate and pitch

4 Tap once on an item to select it (indicated by the black outline) and have it read out. Double-tap to activate a selected item or perform an action

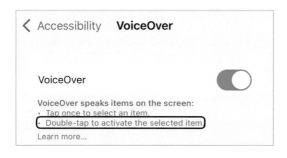

VoiceOver works with the built-in iPhone apps and some apps from the App Store, but not all of them.

Another useful **Accessibility** function is **AssistiveTouch**, within the **Physical and Motor** > **Touch** section. This offers a range of options for accessing items via tapping on the screen, rather than having to swipe with two or more fingers. Tap once on this icon to access items within AssistiveTouch after it has been turned **On**:

177

...cont'd

Zoom settings

Although the iPhone screens are among the largest in the smartphone market, there are times when it can be beneficial to increase the size of items that are being viewed. This can be done with the Zoom feature. To use this:

1 Access the **Accessibility** section as shown on page 176, and tap once on the **Zoom** link

2 By default, the **Zoom** button is **Off**

3 Drag the **Zoom** button **On** to activate the **Zoom** window

4 Drag on this button to move the **Zoom** window around the current screen. Drag with three fingers within the **Zoom** window to move the screen area within it

Drag the **Show Controller** button in Step 4 **On** in the **Zoom** settings to display a control button for the **Zoom** window. Tap once on the control button to view its menu of additional features, such as zooming in for greater or lesser amounts.

5 The **Zoom** window can also be used on the keyboard to increase the size of the keys. As in Step 4 on the previous page, drag with three fingers to move to other parts of the keyboard

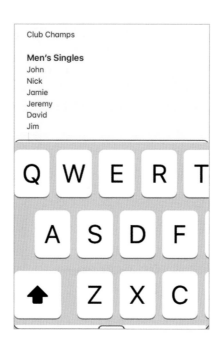

Hot tip

The **Accessibility** settings can also be used to add functionality to the back of the iPhone, by tapping on it. To do this, access **Accessibility** > **Touch**. Swipe up the page and tap once on the **Back Tap** button. Tap once on the **Double Tap** or **Triple Tap** buttons to select options for these actions on the back of the iPhone. Tap once on one of the options to be performed for the double-tap or triple-tap action.

Text size can also be increased within the Accessibility settings. To do this:

1 Under the **Vision** section,

| AA | Display & Text Size | > |

tap once on the **Display & Text Size** link

2 Tap once on the **Larger Text** button

Larger Text

3 Drag the **Larger Accessibility Sizes** button **On** to enable compatible apps to show larger text sizes

4 Drag this slider to set the text size

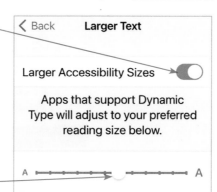

‹ Back   **Larger Text**

Larger Accessibility Sizes ⚪

Apps that support Dynamic Type will adjust to your preferred reading size below.

A •—•—•—•—•—○—•—•—•—• A

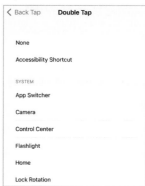

‹ Back Tap   **Double Tap**

None

Accessibility Shortcut

SYSTEM

App Switcher

Camera

Control Center

Flashlight

Home

Lock Rotation

Screen Time

The amount of time that we spend on our digital devices is a growing issue in society, and steps are being taken to let us see exactly how much time we are spending looking at our cellular phone screens. In iOS 16, a range of screen-use options can be monitored with the **Screen Time** feature. To use this:

1 Select **Settings** > **Screen Time**

2 Tap once on the **Turn On Screen Time** button

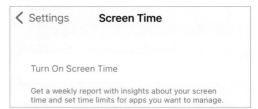

3 Options for using **Screen Time** are displayed

Hot tip

Once **Screen Time** has been turned **On**, it can be turned **Off** again by tapping once on the **Turn Off Screen Time** button at the bottom of the main **Screen Time** window in the Settings app.

4 Tap once on the **Turn On Screen Time** button

5 **Screen Time**
can be set up for
your own use,
or on a child's
iPhone. If it
is set up for a
child, there will
be more parental
control options
for controlling

Is This iPhone for Yourself or Your Child?

Screen Time for a child's iPhone lets you set up additional parental controls.

This is My iPhone

This is My Child's iPhone

the type of content that is available. Tap once on the required option (the same settings can be applied for a child's iPad)

6 The current **Screen Time** usage is shown at the top of the **Screen Time** settings screen. More **Screen Time** options are shown below – see pages 182-183

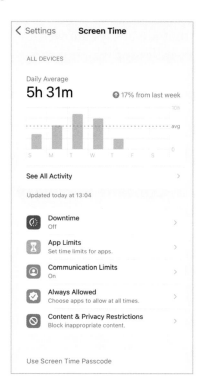

< Settings   **Screen Time**

ALL DEVICES

Daily Average
5h 31m   ⬆ 17% from last week

See All Activity   >

Updated today at 13:04

Downtime
Off   >

App Limits
Set time limits for apps.   >

Communication Limits
On   >

Always Allowed
Choose apps to allow at all times.   >

Content & Privacy Restrictions
Block inappropriate content.   >

Use Screen Time Passcode

Hot tip

If **Screen Time** is set up for a child (**This is My Child's iPhone** option in Step 5), you can create a parental passcode that is required for a child to continue using the iPhone once one of the Screen Time restrictions has been reached.

Don't forget

Each week, the **Screen Time** option produces a report based on the overall usage, as shown in Step 6. The report is identified with a notification when it is published each week.

For each **Screen Time** option, the main Screen Time page can be reached by tapping once on the back arrow at the top of the relevant window.

Content restrictions can be applied for content from the iTunes Store (such as age ratings for movies and TV shows), web content, and search content accessed by Siri, the iPhone's digital voice assistant.

...**cont'd**

Options for Screen Time

Within the **Screen Time** settings there are options for viewing apps and content on your iPhone. Each of these is accessed on the main **Screen Time** settings page.

1   Tap once on **Downtime**

2   Drag the **Scheduled** button **On** and tap once on either **Every Day**, to select the same **Downtime** times for every day, or **Customize Days** to select different times for different days

3   Tap once on **Always Allowed**

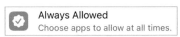

4   The apps that are always allowed to operate, regardless of which settings there are for **Screen Time**, are displayed. Tap once on the red circle next to one to remove it. Select items below the **Choose Apps** heading to add more

5   Tap once on **Content & Privacy Restrictions**

6   Drag the **Content & Privacy Restrictions** button **On** to apply restrictions for blocking inappropriate content

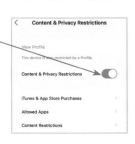

7 Tap once on **App Limits**

8 Tap once on the **Add Limit** button to add time limits for using types of apps

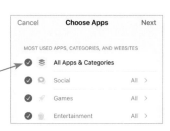

9 Select a category for the types of apps that you want to limit use of (or select **All Apps & Categories**) and tap once on the **Next** button

10 Drag here to specify a time limit for using apps within the category selected in the previous step. By default, this is for each day. Tap once on the **Customize Days** button to set different time limits for specific days

11 Tap once on **Communication Limits**

12 Tap once here to select who can contact you during **Screen Time,** and also **Downtime**, from contacts or everyone

The time limit for using apps is only a suggestion, and the apps do not stop operating when the limit is reached. Instead, a notification appears to alert you to the fact that the time limit has been reached. Tap once on the **Ignore Limit** button to continue using the app.

Select an option for how long you want to ignore the time limit.

Location Services has to be turned **On** to enable the **Find My iPhone** service. This can be done in the Settings app (**Settings** > **Privacy & Security** > **Location Services** > **Find My**) by tapping on **While Using the App**.

If you are using Family Sharing (see pages 70-73), you can use the Find My app to locate the devices of other Family Sharing members. This can be done from your online iCloud account, or with the Find My app.

Finding your iPhone

No one likes to think the worst, but if your iPhone is lost or stolen, help is at hand. The **Find My iPhone** function (operated through the iCloud service) allows you to locate a lost iPhone, and send a message and an alert to it. You can also remotely lock it, or even wipe its contents. This gives added peace of mind, knowing that even if your iPhone is lost or stolen, its contents will not necessarily be compromised. To set up **Find My iPhone**:

1 Tap once on the **Settings** app and tap here

Settings

Q Search

Nick Vandome
Apple ID, iCloud+, Media & Purchases

2 Tap once on the **Find My** button

Find My

3 Tap once on the **Find My iPhone** link if it is showing **Off**. If it is **On** then **Find My iPhone** is already activated

Find My iPhone   Off >

4 Drag the **Find My iPhone** button **On** to be able to find your iPhone on a map

‹ Find My   Find My iPhone

Find My iPhone

Finding a lost iPhone

Once you have set up **Find My iPhone**, you can search for it through the iCloud service. To do this:

1 Log in to your iCloud account at **www.icloud.com** and tap once on the **Find iPhone** button (you also have to sign in again with your Apple ID)

Find iPhone

2 Tap once on the **All Devices** button and select your iPhone. It is identified, and its current location is displayed on the map

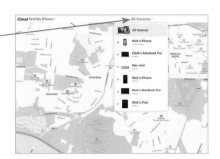

3 Tap once on the green circle to view details about when your iPhone was located

4 Tap once on the **Play Sound** button to send a sound alert to your iPhone

5 Tap once on the **Lost Mode** button to lock your iPhone

6 Enter a phone number on which you can be contacted (optional) and tap once on the **Next** button

7 A message can also be added to be displayed on the lost iPhone. Tap once on the **Done** button to lock the iPhone. It is locked using its existing passcode, which is required to unlock it

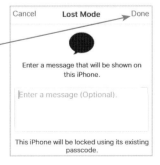

Don't forget

Click once on the **Erase iPhone** button in Step 4 to delete the iPhone's contents. This should be done as a last resort if you think the contents may be compromised. It is important to back up your iPhone to iCloud in case you do ever have to erase its contents. This can be done in **Settings > Apple ID, iCloud, Media & Purchases > iCloud > iCloud Backup** by dragging the **Back Up This iPhone** button **On**. Backups are done automatically when the iPhone is connected to Wi-Fi.

Don't forget

If you have Apple Pay set up on your iPhone, this will be suspended if **Lost Mode** is enabled. It will be reactivated when the passcode is entered to unlock it and your Apple ID is entered within Settings.

Malware is short for malicious software, designed to harm your iPhone or access and distribute information from it.

Apple also checks apps that are provided through the App Store, and this process is very robust. This does not mean that it is impossible for a virus to infect the iPhone, so keep an eye on the Apple website to see if there are any details about iPhone viruses.

Avoiding Viruses

As far as security from viruses on the iPhone is concerned, there is good news and bad news.

- The good news is that, due to its architecture, most apps on the iPhone do not communicate with each other unless specifically required to, such as the Mail and Contacts apps. So, even if there were a virus, it would be difficult for it to infect the whole iPhone. Also, Apple performs rigorous tests on apps that are submitted to the App Store (although even this is not foolproof; see the next bullet point).

- The bad news is that no computer system is immune from viruses and malware, and complacency is one of the biggest enemies of computer security. The iPhone's popularity means it is an attractive target for hackers and virus writers. There have been instances of photos in iCloud being accessed and hacked, but this was more to do with password security, or lack of, than viruses. There have also been some rare, malicious attacks centered on the code used to create apps for the App Store. In some cases, certain apps were affected before the virus was located and remedial action taken. This is a reminder of the need for extreme vigilance against viruses, and for users to check in the media for information about any new attacks. Search the web for "latest viruses" to find websites that specialize in identifying the latest software viruses and threats.

Antivirus options

There are a few apps in the App Store that deal with antivirus issues, although not actually removing viruses. Two options to look at are:

- **McAfee** apps. The online security firm has a number of apps that cover issues such as privacy and passwords.

- **Norton** apps. Similar to McAfee, Norton offers a range of security apps for the iPhone.

Index

G

H

I

K